FROM THE FEAR OF VOODOO TO THE FEAR OF GOD - revised edition

BY

FRANTZ MICHEL

We want to hear from you. Please send your comments about this book and/or testimony how this book has changed your life in care of the address below. Thank you.

P.O. Box 600342
North Miami Beach, FL. 33160

From The Fear Of Voodoo To The Fear of God—Revised Edition

Contents

Introduction

I couldn't think of a better time to write this book. We live in a world where people are confused and uncertain about the future. Many people are doubtful, and fear overwhelms their hearts. Many have turned to the occult, voodoo, or astrology to find answers, but nothing fills the emptiness of their hearts. Vainly they search for answers, and will even lose their souls in the process if they do not turn around and look to Jesus Christ, the ultimate answer to all things.

The problems of this life are so concrete that some feel they do not have the luxury of not fearing tomorrow; while others, such as those who have faith in God, are somewhat optimistic about the future.

Unfortunately, most of the time, the devil comes with his deceitful ways and plants a seed of uncertainty in our hearts and robs us of our joy, hope, and, above all, peace. *From the Fear of Voodoo to the Fear of God* is a thriller that exposes the truth about the demons people are calling angels. It reveals the involvement of the Catholic Church in witchcraft through the practice of Voodoo, and it really explains zombies for what they are, not as the Hollywood movies depict them. This book is a wakeup call for those who are still in the practice of Voodoo or every form of any mystery religion.

There are many people who are involved in demonic activities unknowingly, and there are those who know but are afraid to get out of these evil practices, because they fear the devil might kill them.

I guarantee you, after reading this book; your life will never be the same. I include in it some of my personal experiences in regard to Voodoo and how fear kept me from coming to the "Light" for so long. I also include the experiences of others, such as close family members and friends, who were enslaved by fear of various kinds. In chapter 6 you will read a powerful testimony of a young girl who went to hell and came back and see how God saved her from the fear of the devil and gave her peace.

But there are some very important questions that we need to ask ourselves: What is fear? What is Voodoo? Are zombies real? Can fear stop us from receiving God's blessings in our lives?

Fear is something everyone is familiar with. In every society, there is a small group of people who instill fear in the hearts of millions, perhaps even billions, in order to make their ideas acceptable and to justify whatever they do.

Voodoo, like many other ungodly practices, corrupts and deceives; shame on those who are involved in such things. Voodoo has been right in the backyard of the United States of America since way before I even thought about writing this book. However, people tend to ignore its presence in this land. Yet, a culture and/or a religion can be brought into a land, which was the case for the Caribbean countries and other places that have embraced voodoo. In 1492, Christopher Columbus and the settlers brought Christianity to Hispaniola, now known as Haiti. But their version of Christianity did not bring peace. They used it to oppress the inhabitants of the territory by enslaving them and forcing them to convert to something that brought them pain and sorrow.

Today people in the four corners of the world, whether they are Christians or not, are being driven to embrace ungodly principles. Many governments have passed laws that seem to benefit the population, but unfortunately they are preparing people to welcome the Antichrist. This is a time when you need to keep your eyes open and pray like never before because the devil is more present than ever. He is almost everywhere, attacking God's children. He knows the return of Christ is near, so he is rushing to cause the nations of the world to perish through false doctrines.

Concerning voodoo, the occult, and the world of magic, there are many things that are not being taught in schools of theology. Some pastors will agree with me on this, I am sure. There are many strange things one will discover only from experience or exposure to them.

This is a book that everyone must read—believers, nonbelievers, pastors, and ministers—for you never know where the Lord will call you to serve. You might think that you will never go to a land where people practice voodoo; I am here to tell you that you simply don't know God. Always be ready!

I also explain how your kids in school are exposed to witchcraft. The Internet and television, although entertaining, are sources of distraction, which keep people from focusing on God and can cause your little ones to be misguided and deceived. Sadly, these entertainment media have become parents in some homes. Furthermore, what children are reading in school and learning from some of their friends might be dangerous. Be careful! Music videos and movies are full of subliminal messages luring this generation into evil; some TV commercials are out there to lull people into doing or accepting what is wicked. Be careful for your favorite movie star or music star might be following the following the devil and wants to bring you alone. I encourage you not to follow the crowd or a celebrity but follow Christ.

My intent is not to scare anyone but to warn those who are interested in knowing about other cultures to be careful in their thirst for knowledge, especially when it comes to Voodoo. This is not fiction. The devil is real! If you don't think he exists, you are wrong. Likewise, hell exists, whether you believe it or not, and if you refuse to accept Jesus as your personal Lord and Savior, you are going there. Do something about it! Throughout at the end of most chapters, I give some inspirational notes, prayer and or quotes to think or questions to think about. Do not neglect to read them!

This life brings much stress, and our fears can manifest themselves in various forms. It is up to us to deal with those manifestations so that we do not let our worries bury us alive. After reading this *chef-d'oeuvre*, you will find comfort and ways to overcome your fears so that you can step out in faith and do what God calls you to do. You will discover what the plans of God are for you and that the enemy has no power over you. He cannot hurt or scare you, unless you allow him to do so. You will also learn to differentiate angels from demons, and you will gain profound knowledge of voodoo, particularly Haitian voodoo, and zombies, which is a topic no one has ever talked about in depth as I do in this book.

Share this book with your friends and family. This is a perfect gift from you to them. By giving this book, you are showing that you love them and want the peace of God to dwell in them.

Chapter 1
What Is Fear?

*For God hath not given us the spirit of fear;
but of power, and of love, and of a sound
mind.*

2 Timothy 1:7

One definition of fear is "an unpleasant feeling of
apprehension or distress caused by the presence or
anticipation of danger." I remember back in Haiti, I
heard about a young man who was very strong
physically but afraid of the dark. He was in is early
twenties, and his name was Patrick. One day his
mother, Malia, sent him to buy some candles and
matches; it was about 6 p.m. that day. His brother and
my friend John decided to play a prank on him. In front
of the house was a bunch of trees, so they hid behind
two trees. As Patrick drew near, they made a frightening
sound and shook the trees. Patrick instantly stopped
and froze. Drowning in deep fear, he said without even
reaching his home, "Malia, here are your candles and
matches, Patrick is dead." He fell right on his face after
saying these words. His brother and my friend burst out
laughing. They went out and told the whole
neighborhood.

The prank was dangerous. Patrick could have been
killed; his heart could have stopped. But he did not die
for real as he thought he would. But because of his fear;
he anticipated the danger when there was no actual

one. Christians today are the same; they give up too quickly and easily when faced with life's challenges. They anticipate and invite death in their lives rather than leaning on the Word of God.

Before I go deeper into this, let's look at the different aspects or factors of fear.

There are three types of fear people can have—*by respect, by prudence, and by weakness.* The following examples explain the differences.

"Fear by respect": the child fears his/her mom

"Fear by prudence": the slave fears his master

"Fear by weakness": the sheep fears the lion

Fear by Respect

I was in the ninth grade in Haiti, when one day I decided I was grown up and could do anything I wanted. So I went out walking with a girl I really liked, without telling my mother where I was going to be. It was about 9 o'clock at night, and I still hadn't made it home. My mother and sister were desperately looking for me. Overwhelmed with worries, they went to the morgue, to the local police, and to the home of some friends. There was no sign of me. When I finally showed up at the house, it was about 10:15 p.m.; and I saw superwoman with her whip, eyes red like fire was ready to come out of them. She ground her teeth so hard I could almost see smoke escaping from her mouth.

8

Automatically, I knew what was ahead. Before I began to explain myself, I was already getting hit. And I can tell you that I have never been hit so hard in my life, not even in the martial arts. Was she out of line? Absolutely not! I had violated her principles, and I had to pay the consequences for my actions.

After that day, I never acted that way again, because I respected my mother. I feared her reaction. Today children often talk bad to their parents as if it is OK to do so. Wrong! The Bible is very clear on that: "Children, obey your parents in the Lord, for this is right. Honor your father and mother—which is the first commandment with a promise—that it may go well with you and that you may enjoy long life on the Earth" (Eph. 6: 1-3).

Your parents are your legal guardians; they do not want to see something bad happen to you. It is their duty to raise you well and care for you, and it is incumbent upon you to love and honor them. Most children who disrespect their parents end up doing the same to their spouses, and they have no respect for their elders. That is one of the reasons juvenile delinquency is at such a high level. They carry their own dysfunctional ways into the society, causing many troubles.

But it is not always the children who are to blame for their behavior in society. Parents sometimes are the cause of their children's bad behavior, because of the way they raise their kids. For example, a child who was raised in the fear and admonition of the Lord is more likely to be respectful compared to a child whose parents have rejected the Word of God over some silly voodoo priest or psychic who is not even sure about his or her own future.

Fear by Prudence

"To yield to force is an act of need, not of will; it is at most an act of prudence."[1]

Slavery is not a new term; all of us are familiar with it. One dictionary defines it as "a state of being completely dominated by another." It could be person to person or one nation dominating another. In the land that is now Haiti, history has recorded the many horrifying oppressions, abuses, looting, murders, rapes, and slaughters, among other things, that have occurred throughout the dark time of slavery, when other nations subjugated the territory. Because the slaves were defenseless against the power of the oppressors, prudence was therefore necessary.

Now, *prudence* is a word that comes via Old French from the Latin *prudentia*, a contraction of *providentia*. The Latin word *providentia* means "foresight," which is the ability to envision possible future problems or obstacles or an act or instance of knowing something beforehand.[2]

Slaves did not have freedom of speech or any kind of freedom at all—not even of life. They were considered objects, and their fate was hanging in the hands of their evil masters. For example, according to article 38 of *The*

Black Code" (Le Code Noir) established by King Louis XIV in 1685, in Haiti, or old Hispaniola, if a slave escaped and was caught, the fugitive would lose his/her ears the first time. The second time, he would lose a leg, and the third time an escaped slave was caught, he would face death. Thinking about the consequences of fleeing, the slaves used a lot of prudence, fearing that they would lose a body part or their lives.

The settlers were ruthless and heartless; they were the pure disciples of the devil. In the archives of history is found a letter unveiling the cruelty of the colonists. It was from the French general Rochambeau, who was in Cap Français, known now as Cap Haitian, to his commandant Ramel, who was in Ile de la Tortue. Here is what he wrote: "My dear commandant, I send you a unit of over one hundred fifty men (150) from the National Guard of Cap, commanded by M. Barri with 28 bulldogs with him. I have to let you know not to worry yourself about any ration or any expense for the nourishment of these dogs. You have to give them Negros to eat and their blood to drink. I salute you affectionately. Signed Rochambeau."[3]

Towards the cupidity and atrocity of the colonists, the subjected ones had to take serious precaution, or at least try. Thus, prudence not only was necessary, but it was also crucial.

Today, it is not the colonists who enslave the people of the land but voodoo. Those who live in Haiti and abroad are very prudent with regard to the practices of voodoo, and they should be. Even somebody they do not know may want evil for them and will cast a spell on them just to please the spirits they serve.

Could someone be affected by Voodoo power even if he/she doesn't believe in it?—A: The battle ground is in one's mind. That is why Satan is fighting to occupy it, dwell in it until he destroys you. It is also true that whatsoever you believe in will shape your life, because your thoughts will follow you wherever you go, whether positive or negative. However, your belief has nothing to do with the truth. Fire burns whether you believe it or not. Stick your hand in the fire and you'll get burned. Jump from a tall building and you'll die whether you think you were superman or not. So you may not believe in Voodoo or that it cannot harm you, but I can assure you, if you don't have Jesus Christ as your personal Savior, you are vulnerable. You cannot be neutral in life, it's either you with God or with the devil. If you don't have a protector, Voodoo practitioners can harm you.

Fear by Weakness

At school, many students get bullied because they are or appear to be weak compared to others, especially those who are bigger. The days of the weak ones are like a living hell. School is not fun, and they want to go home, where they feel safe. Sometimes they won't even tell their parents about their torture at school or complain about it to the teachers or the principal. These kids probably will develop anger, grudges, and a vengeful attitude when they grow up. Those angry feelings they carry for so many years can even cause them to commit the most horrible crimes.

Children would not normally grow up wanting to do such evil. Most of the time it is the environment or the people they grow up with who provoke them to act in certain ways. The company you keep has a huge effect on you. If you let your kids hang out with drug addicts, they will end up doing drugs. If they are exposed to violence, they likely will be more prone to act violently. If you teach them voodoo and to fear it, this is what they will carry into their adult years. Exposure can be good or bad, depending on what one is exposed to.

If you are exposed to voodoo and find yourself involved in it, you will not have peace. Torment will always be at your doorstep. There are so many gods to please in voodoo, and no one can please them all. Shame on you if you raise your child in the fear of voodoo instead of the fear of God! Voodoo never brings happiness, but only destruction and fear. Shame on you parents if you give your kids away to voodoo. It is a burden they will have to carry all their lives. They will want to get out of the practice of voodoo, but they won't be able to do so unless they open their hearts to Jesus and let Him take it from there. But sometimes they get so deep they don't even hear the Lord knocking at their door.

As sheep need the protection of the shepherd, we need the help of God for courage and strength when facing tough situations that tend to make us weak and drive us to depression. Many people commit suicide, either because of rejection or because they feel there is nowhere to turn. The devil has many tricks to make you feel worthless and powerless. He want to convince you that there isn't any hope; you might as well give up. He is a liar! Don't be deceived by his conniving ways. When feeling weak and fearful, meditate on this promise from God given to us in Isaiah 41:10: "Fear thou not; for I am with thee: be not dismayed; for I am thy God: I will strengthen thee; yea, I will help thee; yea, I will uphold thee with the right hand of my righteousness."

Biological/ (Physiological) Factor

Fear is one of the greatest obstacles a person has to overcome. When it comes to a point of exaggeration, real problems start rising. When people who can't control their fears come across their phobic objects, their reaction will be spontaneous. At that point, they can hurt themselves or others. I knew a young woman who was afraid of every kind of animal you can name. She was so fearful that even a spider web, without the spider in it, would make her run frantically. She ended up falling many times and injuring herself. If somebody was in her way, she would push the person as hard as she could to escape the perceived danger. But in my opinion she reacted the same many of us would in the presence of things that frighten us.

I remember one day I went to see a friend of mine in northwest Miami. When I got there, I knocked at the front door, and nobody answered. So I went to the back, where I had never been before, to knock. To my surprise I saw a huge dog. I never knew the family owned one and here I was at that time afraid of dogs. Without hesitation, I ran, and the dog started chasing me. I jumped a fence and into the street, escaping from the danger. As I stood in the street, I saw a big sign that read, "Beware of Dogs." I was even more scared, when I realized that I had brought myself into the mouth of that dog.

A couple of days later, I was over my friend's house again, but he was there that time. I said to myself, "Let me try to jump that fence again," because I could not believe I actually had jumped a fence that was that high. I almost broke my neck, when I tried again. You see, fear causes our bodies to release adrenaline, which boosts our strength.

Psychological Factor

Fear can create confusion, weakness, fatigue, hyperventilation, and light-headedness, experts say. Therefore our reactions to fear will be based on instinct.

Perhaps you have heard about the young man who was walking through a cemetery, when suddenly he tripped and fell into a freshly dug grave. He tried as hard as he could to get out, but all his efforts were in vain. That night another man came walking through cemetery and fell into the same hole. He also tried in vain to get out, not seeing the other man. Then the first man said, "You will never get out of here." Instantly, the second man jumped up, got out, and ran!

Fear boosted his energy, and he overcame things he could not have accomplished easily. When you face fear, you can run from it, fight it, or let it keep you prisoner until it kills you. But however you respond to it, your reaction will be spontaneous.

Lack of Experience (Another Source of Fear)

Things that represent great danger for some people cause no fear at all for others. In that sense, fear is subjective. A professional surfer will find it exciting when there are great waves at the ocean and will enjoy the challenge, whereas someone who can't swim will not want to get near the water. He or she may even be afraid to go to a pool because of the fear of drowning.

Some people's fear is the result of a bad experience at some stage of their lives. My late mother's little sister is an example. In their childhood, my mom and my aunt had a terrifying experience. One day they went for a swim at a river in their hometown (Grande Rivière du Nord). As they were in the water, they felt like someone had hold them, but they could not see any hands. Since Haiti is a mysterious land, they automatically knew it must be evil spirits that kept them captive. My mom, being a better swimmer, was trying to use her natural strength to save herself and her little sister, but nothing would work because the demons would not let them go. "My sister was panicked and started to swallow some water," explained my mom. "I saw a stranger, a man in mid ages coming our way. Out of total desperation, I cried for help," she added. "And the man said some words, reached out, and saved us."

After that day, my aunt never wanted to be anywhere close to a river, pool, or ocean. One day when my mom was in her mid-forties, she was swimming in the ocean near our home in Cap Haitian. My aunt yelled, "Don't you learn anything from the past?" The reason she reacted this way was because of the emotional scar left by her past experience with water. Until this day, some forty-five years after that incident, she will not go into the water or come near one a river or the ocean, especially in Haiti, where the voodoo spirits are lurking in the waters.

Besides my aunt, many other people are afraid of the rivers and the seas, simply because of the spirits they believe control these places. They avoid the waters, first, because they can't swim, second, because they are afraid of being bitten by some deadly animals, like sharks, and, third, because of evil creatures (spirits) who lurk in the depth of the waters.

But is fear a sickness? No. It is just a symptom, an emotion. An expert said, "Fear is toxic. It is an emotion, and fear is without a doubt the most toxic of all other emotions." A poison is not a disease, but it can send you to the hospital or to the grave if ingested. Fear does the same thing. Therefore, you can either choose to try to avoid your fear or you can decide to fight it.

Most of the time, the object of our fear is unavoidable. Thus, we will find ourselves fighting it out of necessity.

Take for example those who are in the United States Navy. Before they can think of graduating from boot camp, they have to be at least third-class qualified swimmers. If they cannot pass the swimming test, they will be sent to remedial classes. If they are still unable to meet the Navy's requirements, they will be set back in training, and believe me, no one wants to have that happen to them. Therefore, whether it is lack of experience with the water or fear, it is something they will have to face.

In Navy boot camp, I had several friends from different backgrounds and origins. Some of them struggled in certain areas of training. However, those who could not pass the swimming test were all blacks, whether they were from Africa, the USA, Haiti, or some other place. It was then that I started to believe that most black people can't swim. They call them NQS (nonqualified swimmers). Until they pass, their future in that particular branch of the US Armed Forces is hanging in the balance. But none of my friends let his fear get the best of him. They all overcame their obstacle, passed their test, graduated boot camp, and are now proudly serving their country, here or overseas.

Cultural Factors of Fear

In different countries or societies, there are always things that cause fears, depending on the era. In the US, it used to be that the inequality of blacks and whites created strong discrimination toward the blacks and caused much fear. Black people could not sit in the front of the buses and were mistreated by society, though they were also citizens of the land.

Today, if it's not terrorism that people are afraid of, it's hurricanes and all types of natural disasters. In Florida, it is hurricanes. That is why there is so much hurricane preparedness done throughout the state to help ensure the safety of the residents.

In Haiti the fear is kidnapping. Tourists are afraid to travel over there. Even those who were born in the land are scared to death when the thought of being kidnapped crosses their minds. But this really is not the major issue; voodoo is. Voodoo has been and always will be Haitians' greatest fear. Some Haitians who live in the Diaspora are armed with goodwill to help the people of the land, but they are afraid that if they invest to create jobs that will reduce unemployment, they might see their businesses go down the drain or they might even get killed. And all of this is because of voodoo.

People who live and have kids overseas also are afraid of going back to their homeland (Haiti), because they are afraid that the *loups-garous* ("men-wolves") and evildoers might hurt their children. Of course the land also is not a healthy environment, and they fear that their children will catch a disease or infection, which may be harmful to them, due to unsanitary conditions and lack of clean drinking water. But they are even more afraid of voodoo practitioners, many of whom have some strong demons pushing them to do evil, and children are usually their targets.

Can a nation exist without its culture?

Since Voodoo is part of the Haitian culture, its defenders would always ask the question above particularly when they want to impose their belief on the ones with a different view. Their aim is to make Haitians who reject Voodoo feel guilty or less of a Haitian if they do not embrace their culture.

It is true that a nation has its own customs and traditions which make up its culture. However, losing something, a habit in a culture do not undermine the value of a people in certain ways and whether what is lost affect the people, they still remain a nation.

When I was growing up in the 80's in Haiti, whistling in front of an adult was disrespectful, unthinkable, that's why till this day I can't whistle. Now in this new era, things changed, I've seen kids whistling in the presence of their parents and it is fine with their folks. That which was once considered disrespectful is now accepted. We've lost that value, that sense of respect in our society, but does that exclude us from being a nation? No. And there are many more examples of stuff that we've lost in our culture. Another example, as a tradition, people would go by the river to wash their clothes. Now they start installing new laundry mats in the cities and other places. Imagine a greater percentage of the people stop going to the river to wash their clothes. Would that make them non-Haitians?

What am I saying: losing something in your culture, partly or entirely, do not disqualify you for being a nation. Sometimes, certain things are worth losing to help a nation progress and other times some stuff are worth keeping, especially the positive ones, the ones fill with good morals.

Unfortunately, Voodoo, throughout the years, didn't prove to be up to that good moral standard. Thus, turning away from it will not be a bad thing to do, and I made it clear for you all throughout this book why it is crucial for a change. Don't let anyone fool you, you are still who you are regardless of your choice. You are free and that's one of the greatest gifts that Our Creator has given us. Man is so free that, they can decide to serve God or reject Him. But of course there are consequences to every decision we make. Needless to say, whatever you choose to do that's okay, because you're free. Meanwhile keep in mind that, "everything is permissible, but not beneficial." So you may decide to go with Voodoo even after I opened your eyes or at least tried to do so in truth and in love. Or you can give your life to Christ. If I were you I'd choose the latter.

Voodoo is not to be feared, but not to be underestimated either. The master of Voodoo (ultimately Lucifer) is a ruthless master, he has no love in him; he has no truth in him. He hates God's creation. He has an enmity against the seeds of Israel. Whenever he says a human being, that reminds him of God and because he hates God, he hates you and me. Therefore, to keep in bondage and servitude to him, he uses fear tactics and false promises.

Fear of Uncertainty

Jobs, Schools

With the crash of the economy these days, people are very afraid of losing their jobs. Those who do not have one are fearful about the possibility of never getting one.

In Haiti, where unemployment is outrageous, young men and women are more afraid about their future. They are broke, and they will probably have a family for whom they won't be able to provide. Many have finished high school or college, yet they cannot get a job. It is due to a lack of places available to offer jobs. What is more, the one who is qualified for a position often faces rejection, while someone with no education will come along and fill that particular position even though the person has no clue what he or she is doing.

These conditions have left many youths thinking they have no choice but to quit school early. Because they see little hope of getting a job, they don't want to "waste their time" with education. For those who have finished high school, going to college is another challenge. Most families cannot afford to pay the cost of higher education for their children. In the streets of the major cities of Haiti young adults stand around the blocks doing nothing. In Cap-Haitian, gossiping has become a way of life to the unemployed. Nobody is minding his or her own business. In a particular street of that same city, I know a group of gentlemen who simply take pleasure in watching every female passing by the block and talking bad about them. If one in the group had sex with a girl, when she passes by, he will tell his friends and whoever didn't know about it. If no one in the group had sex with her, they will find something disgusting to say about her just to make themselves feel good.

Many also have become con artists, trying to make a living out of it. They pretend to be voodoo priests; scamming their way to a success that will later destroy them. Fearing God is not in their agenda; they adopt the saying, "Every man for himself." This selfishness is what got Haiti to where it is right now, and this is exactly how the devil wants it to be. Only if we will turn away from evil and live in the fear of the Lord will we experience perfect peace and progress like never before; it's never too late with God!

Relocation

Moving to another location can be stressful. There are several factors one must consider before relocating: cost of living, culture, the law of the land, neighborhoods, etc. No one wants to move to a place and later on regret the move. Relocating is a very big decision, whether it is within a city or a country or from one country to another. Even if all the necessary information is acquired, there is no guarantee that things will be easy. Some people can quickly adapt to a new environment, whereas others may take time to get comfortable to the area and the people within their new community.

Language is also another factor to consider before relocating. For example, an American who does not speak French or Creole will be challenged in Haiti. He or she will always need an interpreter, and a bond must be established between them. Trust will have to be built in their midst. The person translating must be knowledgeable and trustworthy. A bad translation can cause chaos and confusion that can even lead to death.

The fear of uncertainty can be a natural protector. It can motivate us to foresee things and to proceed with caution toward our objectives, be it relocating, going back to school, or obtaining a job. On the other hand, it is a problem when we lock ourselves in the cage of uncertainty and refuse to move forward.

It requires faith to take a big step. But in whom do you have great faith? If it is in you, forget it, for a man doesn't know the desires of his own heart. Is it in some voodoo priest, the occult, or witchcraft? If you trust in these things, the only place you will be moving to is hell.

The only faith that will bring you success is faith in God. The Bible says, "Without faith it is impossible to please God" (Heb. 11:6). If you know all His promises and know that "they are yes in Christ," then you should not be afraid of tomorrow, for He holds it in His hand. All you have to do is believe and trust Him. "In all your ways acknowledge Him and He shall make your paths straight" (Prov. 3:6).

Voodoo practitioners often afraid to relocate from their hometown because they do not want to leave the gods or goddesses of their "*abitasyon*"(a portion of their land claimed by lwas). If situation such as, tough times, financial hardships etc, obliged them to relocate, they will go back at least every year or send someone to bring sacrificial gifts to their gods. One of their greatest fear is not to be able to return back home because the belief in Voodoo is that, certain spell can only be cured by one returning to his/her *abitasyon* and that's the only way they'll survive. Well, if you depend on Voodoo, then what you've thought to believe is true for you.

But if you believe in the one Who gives life, then you might need to reconsider your thoughts. You are seeking protection in the wrong place if you put your trust in Voodoo. Ask yourself: can I add a day in the length of my life? When I die, what does Voodoo guarantee me? Well let me help you: according to the Bible, no one can add or subtract a day in their life. You were created to live in the will of God, but because of disobedience due to our free will, man has decided to follow whatsoever he feels right (keep in mind, by using man I am referring to both men and women).

But regardless on the path you choose, you still going to die one day; death is inevitable. However it is the end of things. Where you are going after death is way more important than your life span here on earth. Well if you have Christ, you are guaranteed eternal life and let's keep it real, when I say Christ, I do not mean profess Him, but possess Him. Furthermore, it's not about having a symbol of Him around your neck, but it is to have Him in your heart. The opposite is also true, if you don't have Him; your life is done and you'll lose your soul for all eternity. The choice is yours. Choose wisely!

Reverence

Another definition of fear is awe or reverence toward God. The Bible says, "The fear of the Lord is the beginning of wisdom: but fools despise wisdom and instruction (Prov. 1:7). Fearing the Lord means: honoring, and being obedient to His Word... for "whoso keepeth not his commandments is a liar, and the truth is not in him" (I John 2:4). Lack of faith is what causes us to doubt. When the winds of trouble blow in our direction, we need to "be still and know that He is God." If we abide in God's love, we will accomplish much. We will not be worrying over every little thing. Worry is associated with fear; in fact, it is another definition for *fear*. When we worry too much, we become like a prey that a predator harasses, seizes by the throat, and makes us feel powerless.

The fourth verse of Psalm 91 says, "His truth shall be thy shield and buckler". This word, buckler can also be rendered as *rampart* from the Latin verb *parade,* "to prepare." When God says something, He usually confirms it in many ways, in different Scriptures. Hence, talking of God's faithfulness in time of trouble, David wrote, "You prepare a table before me in the presence of my enemies; you anoint my head with oil, my cup runs over" (Ps. 23:5). The God of Abraham,

Isaac, and Jacob is a close friend in trouble; He will fully protect you and save you if you call on Him.

Many times we fear because of our material possessions. If we carry large amounts of money, for example, we may be in fear even in the safest neighborhood. There is an adage in Latin: "Cantabit vaccus coram latrone viator," meaning, "The traveler who has nothing will sing while passing in front of the thieves." The Roman poet Juvenal talks about the mortals, who constantly focus on money, and says, "Nothing is more dangerous than the possession of these treasures which already caused many turmoil. If you travel at night with a sum of money, the assassin's knife will frighten you; the shadow of a shaken tree under a bright moon will cause you to tremble, where as the traveler whose pocket is empty will sing while passing in front of the thieves."[4]

The Fear of Death

The fear of death has taken the minds of both believers and nonbelievers hostage. We love our bodies so much that losing them is unthinkable. If, for example, there is a meeting in a room and word comes from the FBI that this room is going to explode in five minutes, I guarantee you that in less than a minute everybody will frantically exit the building.

God has created our bodies so that we can appreciate life. Our brain, for example, is as small as a fist, and yet it can hold more than the content of a library. It is capable of analyzing the flood of information invading it, rejecting what it does not need and keeping what seems to be important. Not only the brain but the eye also is an impeccable work of the Almighty. Even Darwin, author of his idle theory of evolution, after observing the eye admitted that it seemed absurd to suppose that evolution could form the eye.

Throughout time, scientists, philosophers, and poets have tried vainly to understand death. Some became pessimists about life; others embraced the fact that death is unavoidable. Bossuet put it this way: "All calls us to death: the nature so envious... often declares us that it cannot leave us this little matter any longer that it lends to us, which should not remain in the same hands, and which must be eternally in the trade." [5]

Most of the time, we humans are always looking for someone else to blame for our misfortune. Alfred de Vigny, French poet-philosopher of the nineteenth century, thought that God was the source of humans' misfortune. He wrote, "He [Jesus] kneels down, face against the ground; then look to the sky calling: My Father!"[6] The poet was trying to prove that Jesus was abandoned by His own Father. Vigny, like many people of our century, cannot fathom the miracle that happened at the cross. It was the will of the Father to crush the Son so that our sins could be forgiven once and for all.

Alfred de Vigny himself was healed of his pessimism, thanks to religious faith acquired in his last days, argued authors from his time. When there is no hope, people always look for God. Pastor John Hagee said, "When you are down to nothing, God is up to something." Often we fail to understand that the Lord is up there working for our well-being; He is our hope when we have lost everything. But most of the time, we make our plans and try to stick Him in there. However, it should be the other way around.

Again Bossuet, thinking about his substance, wrote, "If I throw sight in front of me, what an appalling continuation where I am not anymore!" David, recognizing the limitation of his life on earth, said in Psalm 39:4-5, "Lord, make me to know my end, and what is the length of my days that I may know how frail I am? Indeed, you have made my days as handbreadths, and my age is as nothing before You."[7]

Although it is true that our lives are measured on earth, it is not the end for those of us who believe in the death and the resurrection of Christ Jesus. A wise man once said, "Our last breath here is our first breath in heaven." Here is the promise from the King of Kings Himself: "Jesus said unto her, I am the resurrection, and the life: he that believeth in me, though he were dead, yet shall he live: And whosoever liveth and believeth in me shall never die. Believest thou this? (John 11:25-26).

The fear of death motivates many who are atheists to acknowledge that there is a God. All their lifetime, they knew that God existed, but they wanted to behave like fools all the while. Why would they talk about Him in the first place if He does not exist? The Bible says of them, "The fool says in his heart that there is no God" (Ps. 14:1). But at the end of the day, when their lives flash before them, they not only confess the Lord's existence but also confess their sin to their fellow humans, hoping to find forgiveness and to enter heaven.

I heard about a man dying at the hospital. His neighbor came to visit him. Agonizing in his bed, he called on his neighbor to come closer so that he could confess his sin to him. He said, "Last year, do you remember when someone broke into your house and stole your big screen TV, and you thought it was the people across the street? Well, it was I. Last month your car got stolen. Again, it was I. And lastly, when your wife cheated on you and you didn't know with whom, I confess that it was I. Now, do you forgive before I die?" And his neighbor replied, "Don't worry, I forgive you. You may die in peace, because the poison that is killing you today, I gave it to you." The moral behind this is that someone is always watching you when you are doing evil. You may think you are off the chain and untouchable, but you are not. One day or another you will have to pay for your actions.

Your Source of Power Determines Your Level of Confidence

If you not only know the Lord by name, but also have a personal relationship with Him, you will be confident that He will protect you and rescue you. For example, as I write, I currently serve in the US Armed Forces. I know that George W. Bush is the commander in chief of America's military. As president, he is making sure the people of the land are well taken care of; he is concerned about their safety. As a member of the military, my job is to "protect and defend the constitution of the United States against foreign and domestic enemies." Do I have a personal relation with the president? No. Does he have power? Absolutely. Although we have the same objectives—keeping America safe and providing humanitarian help to the world—I cannot go to him directly without using a chain of command. My commanding officer cannot go to him as he wishes either. But anyone who can come close to the president will probably ask him for favors, and I am sure he can take care of most of their problems because he has power.

Unlike a human being, it is very easy to have a personal relationship with God. He is your Father. He longs for you to come to Him. He is happy to know that you are depending on Him. Don't be one of those who know Him only by name; trust in Him as well. You do not need a chain of command to go to the Lord. You can have direct contact with Him; and if you do, you will not be in fear, for His perfect love casts out all fears.

Are you facing a great danger, which you think is impossible for you to overcome? Do you need protection? Read the promises of God through King David in Psalm 91 and apply them in your life.

He that dwelleth in the secret place of the most High shall abide under the shadow of the Almighty.

I will say of the L ORD, He is my refuge and my fortress: my God; in him will I trust.

Surely he shall deliver thee from the snare of the fowler, and from the noisome pestilence.

He shall cover thee with his feathers, and under his wings shalt thou trust: his truth shall be thy shield and buckler.

Thou shalt not be afraid for the terror by night; nor for the arrow that flieth by day;

Nor for the pestilence that walketh in darkness; nor for the destruction that wasteth at noonday.

A thousand shall fall at thy side, and ten thousand at thy right hand; but it shall not come nigh thee.

Only with thine eyes shalt thou behold and see the reward of the wicked.

Because thou hast made the L ORD, which is my refuge, even the most High, thy habitation;

There shall no evil befall thee, neither shall any plague come nigh thy dwelling.

For he shall give his angels charge over thee, to keep thee in all thy ways.

They shall bear thee up in their hands, lest thou dash thy foot against a stone.

Thou shalt tread upon the lion and adder: the young lion and the dragon shalt thou trample under feet.

Because he hath set his love upon me, therefore will I deliver him: I will set him on high, because he hath known my name.

He shall call upon me, and I will answer him: I will be with him in trouble; I will deliver him, and honour him.

With long life will I satisfy him, and shew him my salvation.

If you are haunted by fear, know that the only medicine capable of healing you completely is to get closer to God. David found comfort and healing from his fears by seeking the Lord. "I sought the Lord, and He heard me, and delivered me from all my fears" (Ps. 34:4). When fear invades your mind, just seek the Lord and fully trust Him, and He will give you peace. Learn each day to surrender to His love. Keep your focus on Him for at least twenty minutes a day, and you will experience great results in your life. Now, shout these words: "No more worries, no more fears!"

Chapter 2
Haitian Voodoo

Thou shalt have no other gods before Me.

Exodus 20: 3

Today, many nations have turned their backs on God, just as the children of Israel did. Among these is Haiti, a country that has rejected God and embraced voodoo. In this chapter I will be talking about Haitian voodoo and how it has maimed the people of the land of Haiti and what those who are controlled by the fear of voodoo can do to get out of this mess.

Although voodoo originated in West Africa, it is in Haiti that it is most widely practiced and has developed in other forms. The oppressed slaves imported from Africa were obliged to disguise their spirits behind the Roman Catholic saints, a process called *syncretism*, a mixture of West African voodoo and "Christian folk religion." The Africans, most likely the Yorubas people, who serve many gods, did this because they didn't want to lose their tradition and forget their divinities.

The Africans, of course, were not the first occupants of the land, but rather the Indians, the Tainos and the Arawaks, were. But everything changed when Christopher Columbus and his crew set foot in the new territory on December 6, 1492. They enslaved the inhabitants by tricking them and forcing them to accept new religion and other ways of living. Because of the brutality, cruelty, and imported diseases of the settlers, in less than twenty-five years, the Indians were decimated.

The land was rich with pure gold, and the Spaniards were hungry for it. Because of the colonists' greed, there was nothing but fear, pain, and suffering inflicted on the indigenous people. The Spanish exploited all the gold mines of their newfound territory, and when there were no more left, they turned the occidental part of the land over to the French in the Treaty of Ryswick in 1697. The French prospered solely from the production of coffee and sugar in the late eighteenth century, thanks to the forced labor of the slaves brought from Africa. There was an estimated 600,000 inhabitants in St. Domingue (Haiti), 500,000 of whom were slaves. But the Conquistadors started the slave trade from Africa to Hispaniola (Haiti) in the early sixteenth century (1502).[8] Today not only is voodoo a part of Haitian culture, but it is also the religion followed by the majority of the people of the land. To this very moment, many voodoo ceremonies are done in accord with some Catholic Church rituals, because voodoo practitioners are also Catholics.

In the time of slavery, those oppressed felt that their punishments were unbearable. Their sons and daughters were taken away from them; their loved ones were raped and murdered in front of their eyes. A slave was considered property and therefore could be purchased and sold according to the will of the master. Slaves had no freedom of speech. Finally, the slaves turned to voodoo for help. On August 14, 1791, a slave named Bookman, who was a *houngan* (voodoo priest), in a sacrificial ceremony offered a black pig to the devil. Alongside him was a *mambo* (voodoo priestess) possessed by the spirit Erzuli and a known healer among the slaves named Toussaint Louverture. This ceremony was known as the "ceremony of the wood caiman," or *La Cérémonie du Bois Caïman*. It was a blood covenant between the people, through their representatives, and the devil, giving the devil possession of the land of Haiti in exchange for the people's freedom. Historians consider it one of the most important voodoo ceremonies of all time, since it led to the independence of Haiti from the colonists. It was an independence that made Haiti the first free black republic in the history of the world and the second free territory in the Western Hemisphere.

Voodoo Pride, the Cause of Disobedience Toward God

Because in the mind of the Haitian people they got their independence through voodoo, they carry a pride that blinds them and causes the nation to perish. They rejected God and completely embraced voodoo. Some vodouisants actually believe that there is a God; others may have some doubts or don't care at all. Although some may accept that there is a Creator, they still turn to voodoo, because they say that God works too slowly; He takes too long to answer prayers. Therefore, they embrace and worship spirits the voodoo believers think bring faster results. Likewise, there are many people today who turn away from the Lord for the same vile reason; they are impatient. As human beings, we do not know more than the Creator. He knows all our paths and controls our steps. When we leave Him out of our lives, we are driving ourselves right to the pits of hell. Deception, failures, and regrets are the inevitable results.

Sometimes the Most High doesn't answer our prayers. It is not because He hates us but because He sees the road ahead and the danger awaiting us if we get what we ask for. Many times we find ourselves angry at God because things don't happen the way we've planned them. The reality is, if we look back five to ten years, we will thank the Almighty for not letting us get our ways. The Holy Scriptures say: "And not only [so], but we glory in tribulations also: knowing that tribulation worketh patience" (Rom. 5:3).

Contrary to the Word of God, voodoo and other forms of ungodly teaching encourage impatience. The voodoo spirits are always rushing people who consult them to speak up and tell their needs. Usually, the average time they are given by the spirits to see results range from three to twenty-one days. But there is always a catch. Most of the time, what they are asking for comes with a condition. Some have full knowledge of the condition and agree to it no matter what the price, even if they have to give their own children's lives in exchange. Others may not be told of any condition, and they fall right into Satan's trap. They end up losing something or someone dear to them. Most of the time, they will have a miserable until they die. Be careful! Don't become a victim. There are always conditions in voodoo, and they are always harmful.

A Glimpse at the Ceremony of the Wood Caiman or "La Cérémonie du Bois Caïman"

The *cérémonie du Bois caiman* was nothing less than a covenant with the devil by the slaves of Haiti, whereby the people of the land gave to Satan the legal right to possess the territory and the inhabitants for all times. The devil led the slaves to believe that they would be invulnerable to the point that they would not die. But that was a lie! Bookman, the leader and also a houngan, died in battle. The con artist, the father of all lies deceived him and many others.

This covenant was a blood covenant. By sacrificing the black pig, not only did the slaves offer the animal to the devil, but they also offered their own lives to him.

In Haitian voodoo, when one offers an animal to the spirits, he or she is trading its life or the life of a loved one. With the blood of that animal, the spirits claim the lives of whomever they want. The sad part is that practitioners know the truth and still do the wrong thing. They are thirsty for money and power. They believe that only through voodoo can they attain their goals. The devil is always looking for people to carry out his dirty works, and sadly he is been successful through voodoo.

Here's how it works in Haitian voodoo. If you do something to others, they will not seek justice from the court. Instead, they will go to a houngan or a mambo in order to destroy your assets, bring you down to your knees, maim your life, and even kill you. It is "an eye for an eye; a tooth for tooth." Vodouisants seek their own justice and are happy when they cause harm to someone else. There is no peace in voodoo. The same spirit who pretends to warn you of a possible danger or heal you from a disease through a spell is probably the same spirit or "nation"(of spirits) that brought the sickness to your body. All voodoo spirits worship one master, Satan, the great deceiver. Thus, they are not working for the benefit of mankind but are out to destroy our souls, the very thing God loves the most. Open your eyes!

The Spirit Realm in Haitian Voodoo

There are many spirits in voodoo. In the Haitian culture, they are passed on through ancestors. If grandpa or grandma had a spirit who manifested itself in them, 99.9 percent of the time, that same spirit will possess at least one other family member. It could be a grandson, a granddaughter, a son, or a daughter, and the list goes on. It is a curse resulting from the ceremony of "bois caiman." Unless someone in that family accepts Jesus and is baptized, that curse will not be broken. The blood of Jesus Christ is the only cure, because our ancestors made a pact with the devil through blood sacrifice giving him the land and the people living in it for generations to come. But the covenant of God with humans is far greater than this. When He sacrificed His only begotten Son on Calvary by shedding His blood, it was a new covenant signed with mankind to wipe away their sins, break their addictions, free them from bondage, and, above all, give them eternal life for free. In addition, we have the Holy Spirit to guide us, direct us, comfort us, and fill us with the peace of the Father. But voodoo spirits misguide and deceive.

When the voodoo spirits possess someone, it is a full possession. There are no partial possessions; the person being possessed doesn't know anything that is going on or what has happened after the spirit(s) leaves his or her body. People in whom spirits are manifested are called *chwal* (Creole), meaning "horse"(English). This might be because the spirits are able to do whatever they want with that person's body. For example, some people never drink or smoke, but when the spirit(s) takes over, they do all of that and even more awkward things.

One day I was taking part in a voodoo ceremony, and I saw a man possessed by a spirit start climbing a big coconut tree. While the man was at the top of the tree, the spirit said, "He disrespected me by refusing to serve me. I will hurt him." The spirit immediately left his body, and he regained consciousness, but couldn't hold on any longer. He fell from the tree and suffered an injury that incident caused him to be paralyzed to this day.

The voodoo spirits do not play around; they are not your friends. Many times they will be nice to you, but it is just a pretense. They hide their true identity and intentions behind a deceitful mask of goodness. Know this, the devil and his fallen angels, better known as demons, have nothing good in them.

God calls you and me sons and daughters, but the lwas call the **serviteurs** (sèvitè) [servant], horses. Think about it! God Almighty never treats anyone like animal, even those who reject Him. He loves all of us the same way, even the non repented sinners. The depiction of chwal implies that you have no will, that which God has given you is taken away by evil spirits posing as your friends. That is why when they mount a serviteur, it is a complete possession. Just as a horse is forced to do your will, a serviteur is obliged to do the same for the lwas. Serviteurs are considered nothing but properties. Just like a horse, the lwas can dispose of you at will.

But I'll tell you this, you don't have to feel powerless anymore, because you have someone who has all power and authority which have been given unto Him to rule over everything. All you have to do to inherit those promises and have authority over every demon including Satan, is to accept Him as your personal Savior, His name is Jesus Christ, the conqueror of death, hell and the grave. Here is what He is saying to you today: "I have given you authority to trample on snakes and scorpions and to overcome all the power of the enemy; nothing will harm you." (Luke 10:19). That's a wonderful promise that can enable you to face any danger without fear, but first you need to have Jesus as your Master. On the other hand, if Satan is your master the opposite will be true in your life; fear will over shadow you, harm will come your way and soon destruction will follow.

Divisions of Spirits

According to voodoo priests and priestesses, or the spirits themselves that I spoke with when I practiced voodoo, there are twenty-one "nations" of spirits. Some of those "nations" are: Rada, Petwo, Nago, and Congo. But the most worshipped in Haitian voodoo are the Rada and Petwo.

The spirits are called *lwas* or *miste* (Creole), meaning "mystery" (English), *"sen"* (Creole), or "saints" (French-English). They also call themselves *zanj* or *jan'y* (Creole), or angels. Vodouisants (those who practice voodoo), because of lack of education and knowledge, believe these spirits are truly angels, when in fact they are nothing but lying demons. God knew exactly what He was talking about when He said, " My people are destroyed for lack of knowledge" (Hos. 4:6 KJV).

Miste or lwas are divided into two categories: Rada and Petwo. The demons from the Rada are considered to be the good ones. They are only here to heal and protect families, but they can kill if angered. Again, understand that their showing of goodness is just a façade. The Petwos are just another side of the Zanj, whose purpose is to kill and destroy. The most popular term for the lwas of Rada nation is *Ginen*. They are said to be part of the family, and, in the sense, they interacting on a regular basis with the members through their servants.

For example, if someone in the family is sick, a Ginen will show up and heal that person, or it can manifest itself to predict the future, giving warning to the people. But a lwa Petwo is quite different. It is a spirit that one has bought mainly to do evil. That is the belief, but the truth is they are all same; they all worship one master: Satan. Their one and only objective is to find souls to burn in hell with them.

Practitioners always have a strict rule about not mixing Ginen (Rada) with "lwas" (Petwo) because the Ginen side would have people believe that they are not evil. The fact is they are! They hurt and kill people just as lwas of Petwo do.

Every spirit has a name. The most popular ones are the Erzulis: *Erzuli Dantor, Erzuli Freda, and Erzuli Boran.* They are all female spirits. On the male side are *Papa Legba* (Creole) or *Dad Legba* (English). He is the first one to be invoked in every voodoo ceremony. It is said that he is always at the front gates or doors of every house. Then there is the Ogou family: *Ogou Balendjo* and *Ogou Feray,* who operate as military men, or warriors. Another spirit is *Jean Dantor* from the Dantor family. In Haitian voodoo, he is portrayed as a kid, a young shepherd with a staff guarding a flock and highly admired because of his strength. He is celebrated on June 23 and 24 of each year.

Back in 1999 I met a voodoo priest in Cap-Haitian, Haiti by the name Antoine. We called him Uncle Antoine. This man was as scary as his spirits were. He used to live in Port au Prince, the capital city, but he took refuge in the second city after killing over fourteen people with a spell called "expedition" (a voodoo spell designed to kill instantly). He sent it over to destroy some of his enemies. Every person present at that house that day died. This man was heartless. He said, "I am working for the devil, and hell is where I am going." He never cared about his actions. Two things were in his mind, money and doing evil. That man, like some other houngans in Haiti and in the US, serve the lwas from the Petwo nation, the violent ones. If someone serves the Ginen and went on to serve a lwas from the Petwo, he or she would be considered a traitor. It is like abandoning one's own family.

Keep in mind that in some locations of Haiti **zanj** are different from lwas. Even if some people were to use the term *lwas,* they would always say, "Lwas Ginen." The Ginen is specified to distinguish the good spirits from the evil ones, the Petwo. The truth is, both are evil. Don't be deceived! This is how it is: the calm ones (Ginen) are like slow poison; they kill you slowly but surely if you are not under the wings of God. The violent ones kill quickly, like a fatal poison.

While switching sides within voodoo itself is unacceptable, converting to Christianity (Baptist, Seventh-Day Adventist, or other denomination) is worse. Voodoo in this way is like Islam. If you are not with them, you are against them; therefore you should die. They will hurt you unless you truly accept Christ as your personal Savior and abide in His love. God will never allow Satan to destroy His children. Scripture says, "As for God, his way is perfect; the word of the LORD is tried: he is a buckler to all them that trust in him" (2 Sam. 22:31).

A Land of Superstition

Vodouisants consult spirits for anything—for healing, finding love, winning a game, casting a spell on others, protecting a business, and so on. One of the most famous and oldest bands in Haiti, Tropicana d'Haiti, had a song concerning this. Here are some of the lyrics (I am paraphrasing): "They [voodoo practitioners] use superstitions for anything, to win a soccer game, to divide a happy family, to make you say yes even if you don't want, to say no without knowing it. Please God, if you do not intervene your children will perish."

One of the most popular things voodoo practitioners do is to use magic to make people love them. Men do this to women who have disrespected them or those who said, "This man will never have someone like me." Most men who hypnotize the opposite sex do so because they feel hurt and want revenge. After they have sexual intercourse with those girls, they will leave them and let people know what they have done.

Women on the other hand do magic to get a man for the money or to get married, or if their man is gone, they will use voodoo to try to get him back. I have known several women who have done this, and the men actually did come back. But the danger is that the person who puts voodoo on someone to get his or her love won't be happy. The people who search for love through voodoo are always getting abused, beaten, and even killed by their mates. In fact, the lwas always warn them that even though they will get the person back, they should be prepared for some mistreatment; yet they often agree to the conditions.

Because voodoo practitioners believe so obsequiously in superstition, they reject medicine. If their sons or daughters are sick, the first thing that comes to their minds is, "Loups-garous are killing my child." Many of them have wasted their time searching for healing through voodoo when their sicknesses or the ones of their children have nothing to do with magic. Sometimes the houngan or mambo will tell them to go to the doctors, and they won't. Other times, the houngans know that a particular person is dying from natural causes, but he will lie to the family members, telling them the person has been exposed to a spell. They do this so that they can make money off the people. That is why in the end, most people end up dying, and the family places the blame on others.

Don't Blame the Children

Many times I have heard people blaming their kids because of bad grades and making them feel that they are nothing and they will never accomplish anything in life. Stop doing that! Most of the time, it is not their fault that they are doing poorly, but it is the work of the devil. In schools in Haiti, when a child loses his book, his parents always tell him not to take it back if it is found. Why? We have something called *troke tèt,* meaning "exchange brain." Some voodoo practitioners whose kids are lazy in school will have their children steal the book of a classmate, usually the most intelligent one in the class. Once they get the book, notebook, or a page from these objects, they bring it to a houngan or mambo, who will then put a spell on them and instruct the students to go back to class and return what they have stolen, making it look like no one had taken them. If the classmates who lost their materials receive them and open them, they will be under the spell. They will lose their good sense of learning if they are not covered under the blood of Jesus Christ, whereas the lazy kids will be getting all the good grades.

This is why it is so crucial for parents to be under the blood of the King of Kings. Children need protection and guidance. Voodoo will not and cannot give them that. You parents can! And the only way to do this is to break any curse by the power of the Holy Spirit through Christ, the Son of God.

Voodoo Services

Voodoo ceremonies are comprised of drums beating, hands clapping, singing, dancing, and the ringing of a small bell, among other things. There is a master of ceremonies, who prepares a table with all kinds of drinks, flowers, fruits, candles, and images of some spirits. There also have animals for sacrifices. In a small ceremony, like one in a house, the animals will most likely be chickens. They will be of different colored feathers, because each spirit has a preferred color, and to those that don't have a preference multicolored ones are offered. If a spirit kills an animal that is not his or hers, the spirit to whom that beast belongs will be angry when manifested at the service. To introduce the spirits, first greetings are sent to the: *Ontour* (drum) and in second, to *Gran Ximens* (the path leading to the spirit realm) and lastly songs are sung to Papa Legba. This is to ask him for passage at the entrance of the door. He may decide to mount any *chwal,* for any spirit can decide to come first and take part in the service.

Whoever is used to having spirits manifested on them will be possessed at the ceremony, but it is not limited to them. A person who was never possessed before also can be mounted by any spirit, especially if he or she has been chosen since birth. At that time, the spirit will come strong with no discipline because the chwal, or "horse," is not initiated yet. Then a houngan or mambo will use voodoo knowledge to initiate that person in order to calm the spirit down. This will only happen once.

There are occasions when a specific spirit is needed in a service but it cannot be found or come forth because it is busy. No matter how hard the practitioners sing and dance and beat their drums, the spirit will not show up, especially if it is already mad at the person who is doing the service. However, another spirit who already responded to the invocation can live the *chwal* and go down, as they say, into the depth of the ocean and find the spirit needed and bring it forth.

Adaptation: Spirits to Chwal, Chwal to spirit

Although a person may have many spirits, there is always one that is considered the "head." That particular spirit often takes the character, ways, and attitude of his or her "horse." For example, two people can serve Ogou Feray, but the spirit acts differently in each one of them. Usually, spirits like to curse, but if the chwal is a calm individual and doesn't like to curse, then the head spirit will be more or less calm. The opposite is true for someone with a dirty attitude or mouth; his or her spirit will be nasty.

Likewise, if a head spirit is a certain way, then the chwal will get some of his or her traits. The spirit by the name of Jean Laurent is a gay spirit. When a male is possessed by him, that person will act like a homosexual; he will talk like one and make feminine gestures, even when not possessed. When the spirit is manifested, he will mostly do favors to males rather than to females. This is what the Word of God says: "Know ye not that the unrighteousness shall not inherit the kingdom of God? Be not deceived: neither fornicators, not idolaters, nor adulterers, nor effeminate, nor abusers of themselves with mankind, Nor thieves, nor covetous, nor drunkards, nor revilers, nor extortioners, shall inherit the kingdom of God (1 Cor. 6:9-10). Stop and meditate on those verses for a minute!

In Haiti, there are also spirits that patronize specific locations. People from the local place, as well as those from other localities, come to worship and bring gifts to the spirit in that place. In the northern part of Haiti, Grande Rivière du Nord is controlled by Erzuli Dantor or Sainte Rose, Trou du Nord by Jean Dantor or Saint Jean Baptist (Saint John the Baptist), Plaine du Nord by Ogou Balendjo or Saint Jacques Majeur, and this is just a few. A spirit or saint can patronize more than one city. For example, Notre Dame du Perpetuel Secours, who is worshipped as the Virgin Mary, is the patron of Haiti and celebrated on the August 15 each year in locations such as Cap-Haitian, Les Cayes, Petit Goâves, and Ouanaminthes.

In a remote location from the second city (Cap-Haitian), there is a place called Picolet, which is a stronghold for spirits. There vodouisants find almost all the Ginen spirits. It lies on top of a mountain, above the ocean. Practitioners go there every day to worship, but they are in greater numbers on Tuesdays and Fridays. In voodoo, those days are considered powerful.

Picolet is a spooky place. I have been there several times. There is a corner for each spirit. Practitioners go directly to the spirit(s) they need. Sometimes voodoo ceremonies are conducted there. The ocean beneath Picolet is guarded by a demon called La sirène. She is the queen of the sea. All boats departing Haiti must pay a price to her. It can be some flowers thrown into the ocean for her or a bottle of alcoholic beverage. But it is not limited to these things. She can decide to ask for any types of gifts. If a follower doesn't give the required gift, his or her ship could be destroyed forever. The debris of a freight ship has been lying at the shore of Picolet for over fifteen years. Because its owner failed to pay his debt to the spirit, she caused the boat to have an inexplicable problem and perish on site.

There is another place called Galman du plat, governed by a spirit called Lovana. She lives in a basin called "Basin of Lovana." When she wants to, she shows herself to people by taking the form of a fish wearing an earring. When vodouisants go to offer animal sacrifices to her, she sometimes takes those animals alive, especially if they are goats. She instructs her followers to tie a noose around the beast's neck and bring it to the water. She then takes it and leaves the rope.

One of the most celebrated spirits in Haiti is Saint Jacques Majeur, also known as Ogou Balendjo or Parenn Ogou (Godfather Ogou), as voodoo practitioners call him. Each year, on July 24, people (pilgrims) come from all the nine departments of Haiti and in the Diaspora to celebrate "La Saint Jacques"(The Saint Jacques). People come by the busload, and airplanes arrive filled with those living abroad. That is why airline companies raise their prices at that time of year, because they know for sure that many will go to Haiti in greater numbers from June until early August.

Before and throughout the festivity, those who were helped by the spirit in any way bring gifts to him and bathe in a nasty, muddy, filthy, and stinking hole called "Bassin Saint Jacques." The belief is that the bathing brings them more luck. The place is gross. Just looking at people in the mud pot will make you want to throw up, and yet people are enjoying it. In my years in voodoo, I never bathed in it. Would I have done it if I were still practicing voodoo? The truth is yes. Voodoo brainwashes it adherents, and because of fear subjects them to doing anything the spirits ask.

Unveiling the Rada Spirits

Although Rada nation is known for the calmer spirits, there are many of them who do not exhibit that calmness. For example, Laila, a female spirit from that nation, hates children! If someone is possessed by a lwa and that spirit decides to invoke *Laila* to take over, the people around are advised in advance not to let any children too close, or she will hurt them.

Anse A Foleur, in the northwest part of Haiti, is where vodouisants go to seek revenge from *Ti sentann,* or Petite Sainte Anne (little Saint Anne). She is known for bringing justice, but how? She quickly kills with no questions asked. Those who love doing evil go there for faster results, and it doesn't cost them a fortune. They say if they go to a houngan to kill someone, it is way more expensive than it is to go to little Saint Anne. I have met several people who reported the works of that spirit. Among them is an old friend from Cap-Haitian who said this: " I went to little Saint Anne because someone slapped me. The next morning when I got home from Anse A Foleur, I heard of the death of that young man who insulted me."

I know some followers still think of voodoo as a good religion and/or culture, believing that it is of God. I am here to tell those of you who believe this, that it is from Satan and not from the Most High. The practices of it are contradictory to God's Word. Spirits who murder human beings and hate children cannot be of the Lord; He doesn't create to destroy His own.

Which side are you on, the good or the bad? I hope it is the good. If not, turn around and join the winning team because God will never fail you; He is faithful to His promises.

Parallels and Contrasts Between Houngans and Mambos

Neither priests nor priestesses are limited to the amount of lwas that can manifest in them, Rada or Petwo. Both kill, and they worship the same master: Satan. They can't get along with one another because of pride; it is houngans versus houngans, houngans versus mambos, and mambos versus mambos. Each one always thinks he or she has the more powerful lwa. Thus, they are always testing each other by casting out spells on one another. Deaths usually result from these spiritual attacks, and those who die from these fierce attacks get turned into zombies.

Although they may have many lwas from both Rada and Petwo, houngans are more into the Petwo lwas, whereas the mambos are more into the Rada. Houngans love to serve the deadly lwas more than the voodoo priestesses. One of the most popular lwas the voodoo priests love to serve is called *Criminel* (French), or *Criminal* (English). He is an evil, powerful spirit who loves to drink blood. He does not give second chances; if you are not with God, he will get you.

Houngans love to have many concubines, although they may have one wife, and all these women live in the same house. Most of the time, they are afraid to leave, even to escape mistreatment, because they can get killed by magic and turned into zombie to serve as a slave. Mambos, on the other hand, do not live with many in their houses, but they have many boyfriends, even when they have a husband. They are not faithful to their men, just as the houngans are unfaithful to their women

Parallels and Contrasts Between Gideon and Bookman

Both the biblical Gideon and Haiti's Bookman experienced tribulation. Their people were facing oppression and crying out for justice in the midst of the abuse. God chose a cowardly, but not prideful, Gideon to lead an army reduced to three hundred men to save the Israelites from the Midianites (Judg. 7:7). They were greatly outnumbered, but God saved them, giving them victory over their enemies. Gideon and his army came out the battle unharmed.

Bookman, on the other hand, was chosen by the devil, to whom he sacrificed a black pig, and everyone with him drank the blood of the animal. They did so in order to be invulnerable. About one week after the ceremony, they started an uprising, killing as many as one thousand whites and burning their properties. Unfortunately, the spirits were not faithful to their promises; Bookman, the leader, was killed in combat.

I value our freedom and respect the brave slaves who sacrificed their lives to make us independent today. But it is time that voodoo fanatics stopped being prideful and recognized that there is only one true God, the great "I Am." A nation that rejects God to honor other gods will not prosper. Haiti will not see progress until the nation turns to the Lord. Many gods deceive, destroy, and bring confusion, but the only true God brings peace, love, and healing for the brokenhearted.

Haiti and Israel

Haiti and Israel, like no other countries, have suffered atrocity and cruelty at the hands of many nations. The people were enslaved and treated like objects that didn't have rights, not even to life. Their masters decided when they lived and when they died. Thus, both the Jewish people and the slaves of Haiti were killed in great numbers. The Jews were scattered around the world, yet God gave a breathtaking prophecy to the prophet Ezekiel about the rebuilding of the State of Israel. In Ezekiel 37 the prophet saw "the valley of dry bones." The dry bones came together and were covered with skin (vv. 7-8), God then breathed His life into them. Ezekiel wrote, "So I prophesied as he commanded me, and the breath came into them, and they lived, and stood up upon their feet an exceeding great army" (v.10).

On May 15, 1948 the State of Israel was rebuilt in one day. This event also was predicted by the prophet Isaiah, when God said to him, "Who hath heard such things? Shall the earth be made to bring forth in one day? or shall a nation be born at once? For as soon as Zion travailed, she brought forth her children" (Isa. 66:8). A country with centuries of mistreatment and genocide, from the Crusades to Hitler's Holocaust, now has one of the world's elite military and intelligence service. As amazing and accurate as the prophecies of Isaiah 66:8 and Ezekiel 37 are, they are no surprise to those that believe in God, for they know all His words are true.

The land of Israel is for the Jewish people forever. God gave it to them. Though they were dispersed, the Lord brought them back to it. He told Ezekiel, "Therefore prophesy and say unto them, Thus saith the Lord GOD; Behold, O my people, I will open your graves, and cause you to come up out of your graves, and bring you into the land of Israel" (Ezek. 37:12).

Haiti defeated the best army in the world (the French army of Napoleon Bonaparte) to gain her independence. History records that they did this with little equipment but with the help of voodoo. But today, Haiti has no military power or military personnel present at all. From 1993 to 1998, there were some regions in Haiti that didn't have military or police forces present, because after the dissolution of the Haitian armed forces, the newly graduated police officers in June of 1995 were less than 3,000 for a population of nearly 10 million.

As an ex-police officer myself, I know that it wasn't until 1997 that we opened the police station in Milot, a city located near the second city. Before we came there, the population had their own prisons and law, and they mistreated one another. There was no structure among them. Abuse and injustice were reported in several locations of Haiti because of the scarceness of officers.

Independence was supposed to create union, but greed and thirst for power caused betrayal among the people of the new republic. Dessalines, the father of Haitian independence and emperor of the land was assassinated at Pont-Rouge on October 17, 1806 in an ambush only two years and nine months after he proclaimed independence. Today again, politicians are killing each other over power and money. The land is divided; there is no peace, no union. Political parties are as numerous as anthills, and not one of them is looking to save the country; they are only seeking to fill their pockets. Some heads of state have made declarations that led the population to act foolishly. In a country like Haiti, where the majority of the people are illiterate, there are statements you simply do not make as leaders. The current president of Haiti, Rene G. Préval, on his first mandate in the 1990s stated, "*Naje pou ou soti*," meaning, "Do whatever it takes to help yourself." As a representative of the people, he was just saying that the solution to their problems had nothing to do with him as the executive.

After that statement, people began looting businesses; burglaries were reported in many areas of the country, and the assailants quoted the president's words each time they committed an act of stealing. The truth is, the commander in chief's words were a key to opening the doors of immorality and foolishness.

Popular president of Haiti Jean Bertrand Aristide encouraged the population to give "Père Lebrun" to the Haitian armed forces personnel. Père Lebrun, if my mind serves me right, was the name of a tire shop owner. Aristide used that term as a metaphor for asking the mass population to burn alive the military members, using tires, gasoline, and matches as weapons. Many people lost their lives. They were beaten, had their private parts cut off, and were burned alive with tires and gas at the hand of the population. I can't say that the military men were all angels; some had used their power to abuse the population. But the words of the president encouraging the people to commit those murders were crueler than any crimes that occurred during the time.

This is purely satanic! Furthermore, as a Roman Catholic priest at that time, moral standards and compassion were supposed to be his creed, but he proved the opposite. In addition, it was in the government of Jean Bertrand Aristide that voodoo was recognized as a religion in April 2003.

From the ancient times before Christ until now, mankind has been disobedient to God. One of the most ungrateful acts from man toward the Most High was in the time of Moses. The book of Exodus records the atrocity, brutality, mistreatment, and injustice done to the people of the Lord. As a good Father, God intervened. He used Moses to deliver His people out of slavery and bondage to the Egyptians. Jehovah said to Moses, "Come now therefore, and I will send you unto Pharaoh, that thou mayest bring forth my people the children of Israel out of Egypt" (Exod. 3:10).

Pharaoh refused to let the people go, and his heart was hardened. After many attempts from Moses, the king still did not change his mind. God had to send a final plague, the plague of the death of the firstborn. The Lord instructed Moses on how to protect his own from that plague, and the Bible tells us, "And it came to pass, that at midnight the LORD smote all the firstborn in the land of Egypt, from the firstborn of Pharaoh that sat on his throne unto the first born of the captive that was in the dungeon; and all the firstborn of the cattle" (Exod. 12:29). This caused Pharaoh to let the children of the Lord go (v.31).

When God makes a promise, He will keep it and make sure that it comes to pass. He is too wise to make mistakes and too faithful to be unjust. But what of us? We need to be obedient and fully trust God. The children of Israel did the opposite. They turned their backs on God and made other gods for themselves and bowed down to them, even after the Almighty instructed them not to. That was a direct violation of the second commandment. Here what the word says concerning the unfaithfulness of the Israelites toward The Lord in Exodus 32:1: "When the people saw that Moses was so long in coming down from the mountain, they gathered around Aaron and said, 'Come, make us gods who will go before us. As for this fellow Moses who brought us up out of Egypt, we don't know what has happened to him.'" God was so angry at that point that He wanted to eradicate the people from the face of the earth. But for the sake of His covenant with Abraham, Isaac, and Jacob, He did not hurt them.

Is there such thing as good and bad voodoo?

There is no such thing. As a religion, it is either you are all good or all bad. Now we know that many crimes have been committed in the name of religion. Man was created free, even after sinning; we still possess the ability or the freedom to choose. We can make our own gods and decide not to follow Christ. People always want answers and they want them now. Mancan impose their belief on another fellow human because of our sinful nature. And this is where wisdom will come in handy to discern. Your religion should be your relationship with your leader. If you're a Christian, then follow Christ. If you're a Muslim then follow Mohamed and so on. Should we call an un-repented murderer, liar, adulterer Christian? No. if you don't see yourself repenting to God, then that's proof that you're not a Christian. Thus, I prefer a close intimate relation with my God, the God of Abraham, Isaac and Jacob than a title.

Consequently, if you're a voodoo practitioner, you will have to abide or play by their rules. Throughout all my years exposed toVoodoo, I never see a book that sets a guideline for practitioners, thus everyone follow their own heart. And as per the Bible, we know that, "the heart is deceitfully wicked." That is why revenge is the number one creed of a voodoo believer or practitioner, totally the opposite of God's word. I've heard people say that Voodoo is a beautiful religion if people could understand it. That's psychology, beautiful words, but no substance. What is there in voodoo to understand, deeper you get, the more confuse and wicked you become. How would you learn something with word of mouth? By the time it gets to the 7th person in a crowd of a hundred, the essence of what was said will be lost, the sentence will not be the same, I can assure you. Just one sentence will be lost, try it and you'll see. Now imagine a bunch of sentences (unwritten) passed down. You see the confusion! And mind you it is done on purpose. God the Omni Potent has to write His commandments, not only said but written for us.

In other words, although I refrain from siding for a religion, I will say, after careful consideration, that Christianity, if the guidelines prescribed by Jesus are followed to the letter, will be a beautiful religion; a religion based on relationship.

With Voodoo is do as you please. Someone takes your stuff, kill him if it pleases you. Someone doesn't want to marry you, make them marry you with magic regardless if you'll divorce him/her later. Someone do you wrong, kill him and turn them into a zombie if that's what will make you happy. Pay back is what Voodoo goes by. Now dear reader, you tell me what's so good about a religion like that? Remember you are following your heart. Every voodoo practitioner knows exactly what I am talking about. But some of you will tell me, "what about when someone is sick and a spirit comes and heals him, isn't this good voodoo?" if you're looking at it n one side, yes. But let me open your eyes even if you are a voodoo practitioner who was unaware of what I am going say, trust me there are many who are unaware of certain things. When you are sick through a spell, it is usually the same spirit or his/her acolytes who caused that sickness to your body. Then they come and heal you, making you believe that they love you and if you want to stay alive, you'll have to follow them meaning worship them as "your god." Imagine a doctor who poisons you without your knowledge, but he also has the antidote that can cure you. Is that a good thing for him to put through all the pain that you didn't ask for, then to rule over you he comes and heals you? You be the judge!

Can Voodoo help Haiti?

The answer to this question is simple: No. something that is used to destroy its society can in no way, be of help. Defenders of Voodoo will always say that it is the people who use it to do wrong or evil, but they never have a meeting among tem to turn this around. Why? Because they know that this is impossible. First of all, they do not have any rule book by which they go by; no written laws that structure their religion. So it is always total mayhem, one will always trying to rule over another. Second, Voodoo has to many gods to please and voodoo practitioners can agree with me on this. Too many things to do or too many people, spirits to please creates confusion. Third, even if they were to call on the saint patron of Haiti, ErzuliDantor (Our lady of perpetual help), that wouldn't help. Where is she all that time? The nation refuse to understand, her job is done. All she wanted was the dedication of the land to her, nothing more.

She is not a savior, she loves the condition Haiti is in right now. You may be asking, why God doesn't help either? That's a fair question. As powerful as He is, God cannot help Haiti if we blatantly reject Him. The nation is not ignorant of the existence of Jehovah, but they refuse to follow the rules of their Maker. The Lord states in II Chronicles 7:14, "if the people that are called by My name will humble themselves and pray, then I will hear from Heaven and heal their land." How many see the conditions here? The people have to humble themselves and pray. By doing so, God Himself will come down and deliver us.

It is time that we set aside pride, jealousy, boastfulness that's eating the country alive. It is time that we reject these deaf gods and humble before the One true God, this is the only way Haiti can be saved. Haiti's help will come from the Lord Almighty. Any other attempt or route will be in vain. We've been trying with Erzuli since 1804 after the independence, nothing works. Now, why don't we try with God? And don't use excuses like, "we are also Catholics, we pray to God. No, you pray to your "god," the Virgin Mary or whichever spirit you worship. If you're serious about following Christ, do so in spirit and in true as He commands it.

Today that same God wants to show mercy to you who are practicing voodoo. Will you be obedient to Him? If you obey, it will be a blessing to you and your children and their descendants. Voodoo cannot save you from the eternal fire; in fact, it can cause you to go there. In short, those who practice voodoo need to turn away from it and embrace the gospel of Jesus Christ, because He is the Light of the World and eternal life to those who come to Him!

Some Voodoo Terms to Know

Lwas: Evil voodoo spirits

Houngans/Bokors: Voodoo priests (fully initiated), one who has received the "Asson."

Mambos: Voodoo priestesses (also fully initiated).

Asson: The sacred rattle of Voudoun

Chwal or Serviteur (French), *Sèvitè* (Creole): Practitioners whom spirits (Lwas) mount

Badjikan/Hounsi: A voodoo priest want-to-be. lwas don't mount them, but they serve the houngans and mambos. He/she is a devotee at the honfour

Vodouisants: those who practice voodoo

Maman Brigitte: she is also called Grande (Grandmother) Brigitte; she is the female "Guardian of Graves." She is a powerful magical Loa or Lwa and wife of Baron

Baron: Guardian of the cemeteries.

Honfour/Peristyle: altar, the inner sanctuary of the Hougan or Mambo.

Chapter 3
Voodoo and the Catholic Church

Nevertheless, the foundation of God standeth sure, having this seal, The Lord knoweth them that are his. And let everyone that nameth the name of Christ depart from iniquity.

2 Timothy 2:19

In the past, the Catholic Church and voodoo did not get along; the church persecuted voodoo practitioners for years. Why do they now get along? Is the Catholic Church the light of the world, as many think?

Whenever there is light, darkness cannot prevail. Imagine a very dark room. While inside, you are unable to see where to go, you might even hurt yourself trying to find something, for you will be stumbling everywhere you attempt to go. Furthermore, if you are afraid of the dark, you'll probably not even attempt to go inside at all. Light is very important. It is needed to operate a car at night; without it many more accidents would have occurred, leaving many casualties. Without light, life would be very difficult. Imagine the US without electricity for a year. Industries would stop functioning, and people would lose their jobs, leaving most families in desperation. People would starve in their homes.

Voodoo was persecuted by the Catholic Church because it was considered darkness and evil. Now, the two are coexisting. The Catholic Church showed weakness toward voodoo. If the church now works in harmony with voodoo, this proves that it was not light in the first place.

It should not be shocking to hear that Haitian voodoo and the Catholic Church work hand in hand. It is not the first time in history that we find the Roman Catholic Church involved or promoting something ungodly.

In an article dated April 17, 2002, Bill Press (Tribune Media Service) reported how silent the leaders of the Catholic Church were in the cases of several priests raping young boys. Here are some paragraphs from the article.

> There was, first, the case of Father John Geoghegan, recently sent to prison, no thanks to Cardinal Law, for molesting hundreds of young boys. Instead of reporting him to law enforcement authorities, Law and his predecessor transferred Geoghegan from one parish to the next—and his next set of victims.

> But the story of Father Paul Shandley is even more shocking because his sexual depravity was public knowledge, and because he's still on the loose.

> According to diocesan records released this week, church officials knew as early as 1967 that Father Shandley had molested at least one little boy, whose name, address and

phone number were included in church files. He was suspected of abusing several others.

The file also contains a report on Shandley's attendance at a meeting of the North American Man Boy Love Association, at which he stated that "a boy was actually helped by a man/boy love relationship." He only suffered, said Shandley, when forced to report the incident and undergo therapy. At a second NAMBLA meeting, also documented in his official file, Shandley asserted that whenever adults have sex with children, it is the children who seduce the adults.

Armed with such damaging evidence, what did Cardinal Law do about Shandley? He didn't turn him over to the police. He didn't punish him. He rewarded him! Named him pastor of a suburban Boston parish in 1985. Five years later, amid more reports of child abuse, he granted Shandley sick leave, while the archdiocese continued to pay his salary, living expenses and medical bills. Shandley and another priest, also on paid leave from the Boston Archdiocese, used the money to buy a gay resort in Palm Springs.[9]

You don't need to be religious or have a bachelor's degree to know that this is wrong and wicked. Let me take you way back in history when Hitler, under the blessing of the pope of his time, killed 6 million Jews.

Still earlier, the crusaders claimed the lives of thousands of innocent people. This is just to name a few of the crimes committed under the name of religion, ordered or approved by the popes of the Catholic Church. History recorded that more than 100 million people have lost their lives because of the cruelty and animosity of the Catholic Church.

There were nine crusades, some of which were ordered by the popes, while the rest were approved by them. History records that the first crusade, November 27, 1095, was ordered by Pope Urban II. He ordered that the heretics be tortured or killed. In 1096, as many as12,000 lost their lives. In July 1099, the crusaders killed 20,000 men, women, and children. In that same year they claimed the lives of 30,000 people. The second crusade was ordered by Pope Eugene III in 1147-1149, and the third one by Gregory VIII. This is just to name a few. In total, the nine crusades claimed the lives of about **56,000,000 people**, Christians, Jews and Muslims.[10]

What could be more evil and wicked than that? Again, this is not a surprise if voodoo and the Catholic Church are now sisters. When the settlers invaded the land of Hispaniola, now Haiti, they pretended to come in peace, but later on they showed their evil side by enslaving the inhabitants of the land. They offered Christianity but only with the intent of controlling the people through the religion they imported into the new territory. Even though they were forced to follow the rules of the Catholic Church, the slaves continued to have private meetings and syncretized their gods with the Catholic saints. Today most vodouisants go to the Catholic Church and pray to the saints. But why do they go to Catholic Church?

Each parish has a so-called "saint" who resides in it. (In this chapter, I speak only about the ones in Haiti.) Who are the saints of the Catholic Church? Are they really what people think they are? In his book, *Rescued from Hell*, Bakajika Muana Nkuba, a man who had a direct encounter with Lucifer in the invisible world explained this.

> Each saint in the catholic repertory, whom Rome uses to seduce the entire world, is not a saint in the real sense of the word. These are dead people of often doubtful origins and lifestyles who are venerated by Catholics. Many of them have been magicians or Rosicrucians serving the devil while living. The bodies are then mummified, just as for the Popes, and kept in the vaults of saint Peter's Basilica.

> When a new parish is opened somewhere, all of these spirits assemble together in the invisible world and draw lots to know which saint will be assigned to it. Once a name has been chosen, Lucifer orders the Pope to remove a piece of the body of this person. The part is then prepared by being enclosed in a white-colored stone which will be placed

inside the new church's altar. From now on it is that particular demon who will patronize all of the activities of the parish."[11]

Many years ago, a similar thing was about to take place. When Moses died, Lucifer tried to get his body in order to turn it into a shrine so that people of the world might come and worship Moses. But God sent his archangel Michael to prevent Satan from accomplishing his goal. "Yet Michael the archangel, when contending with the devil he disputed about the body of Moses, durst not bring against him a railing accusation, but said, The Lord rebuke thee" (Jude1:9).

In Haiti, each Catholic Church is represented by one of the voodoo spirits from the Rada nation, also called saints. They are carved images placed inside the church. People who practice voodoo and/or are polytheists come to worship them and praise them for miracles, thinking they are the solution to their problems. These lost people think that these so-called saints are of God and that it is fine to bow down to them. False! They are being blinded and deceived by the Catholic Church.

In a particular suburb in the northern part of Haiti, Bord de Mer de Limonade, the parish there is patronized by a spirit named Sainte Philomène, or Manze Philomise for her voodoo name. Her favorite colors are white and turquoise blue, or pink and white in some other areas where she is also worshiped. It is believed by practitioners that she died very young at the age of 19. She is from the Rada nation in the spirit realm. In the picture representing her, she is standing next to an anchor. Her displayed statue in the local Catholic Church was found by a fisherman. A long time ago he went on a fishing trip. When he cast his net, he felt that he had caught something heavy, probably a big fish. He quickly pulled in the net, and surprisingly it was the image (statue) of Philomise. He threw the image back into the ocean and drove his small boat miles away. He cast his net a second time, and he caught the same statue that he had dropped a great distance away from his new location. He dumped her again, and this time he drove his boat farther away. When he cast his net, the same thing happened. This time, he took the image and brought it to the local Catholic Church. The priest in charge of the parish took the statue, blessed it, and placed it in the church until the present day.

Philomise is very powerful. She is half fish (cod, her bottom) and half human (a beautiful white woman, the top). In Haitian voodoo, she is also called *La sirène* (French), or "mermaid" (English). She is known as the queen of the sea, which is probably the reason she is portrayed with the anchor. This demon controls the prostitutes. In fact, her lower part, "cod," is *morue* in French; this word is also used in a pejorative way and translated as *tart* in English, meaning, "promiscuous woman, prostitute."[12]

She is celebrated on the fifth of September each year. On the day of her celebration, the man who found the statue goes on a fishing trip, and no matter how many fish he catches that day, he gives them away to people of the area. In honor of that "demon," he painted his boat in white and blue and named it *Sainte Philomène*.

I have seen this image worshipped. In fact, in my years of voodoo, I worshipped her also with my gifts and offerings. I brought flowers to her and deposited them at her feet, just like everybody else who worships her does, not knowing I was praising a deaf goddess, a creature who couldn't care less about my problems. When you are praising a saint, you are honoring the spirit of a dead person, which is an act condemned by God.

There is another powerful spirit in Haitian voodoo called Damballa, or Damballah. He is a snake lwa; and in the Catholic Church, he is represented by St. Patrick (Petwo rite) and St. Moses (Rada rite). He is very crafty and has a double sex. Furthermore, as St. Moses, voodoo practitioners from West Africa and the Diaspora associated him with the symbol of the rainbow, the serpent deity, or Damballa. He is powerful and sometimes even worshipped as a god. As a male, Moses in some locations means "savior" and as a female means "muse."

In Haitian voodoo, Damballa loves to marry women (see chapter on marriage) and have sex with them. There are many people in Haiti who have reportedly left their girlfriends or wives because they surprisingly saw them lying in bed with a big snake (damballa). In most cases, the snake is inside their private parts, but

Damballa also can take a human form to have sexual intercourse with them. Many female voodoo practitioners cannot become pregnant, and it is because of Damballa. Having sex with this demon provokes diseases such as fibroid, uterine cancer. Of course, not all women who have had or have these diseases suffer them as a result of this spirit.

The Guédés

The *guédés* are spirits of the dead, celebrated in November. Their favorite food is hot pepper and heavy liquor. At time of the guédés, Rada spirits do not manifest themselves except in extreme emergencies, as when someone has been exposed to a deadly spell. Otherwise those who do not mix their Rada with Petwo will have to wait until after November to see their favorite lwas. Even though only lwas from Petwo manifest on guédés, most vodouisants still go to the cemeteries to worship the dead. First, they go to church (Catholic). Then they go to the place where the dead rest with candles lit and food and liquor to pour out to their loved ones.

When a loved one dies, family members, under the influence of voodoo spirits, must have a mass celebration in order to send away the departed soul in peace. The belief is that the dead will be tormented if this is not done for them or that their spirits will come back to torment their families. This is a trick to make you worship the dead. Don't fall for it! Because the voodoo spirits know you love your parents or children, they entice you to do the opposite of God's Word. There is only one way I have seen in the Bible for one's soul to be at peace. You must know Jesus Christ as your personal Lord and Savior, or you'll lose your soul. Don't let Satan fool you; he just wants company in hell!

Fête des Pèlerins (Festival of the Pilgrims)

In Haiti, each city or suburb has a different date for celebrating the spirit that patronizes that specific place. On these occasions people from everywhere, from across Haiti and the Diaspora, come in huge numbers to worship the saint(s) who helped them the most. They bring flowers, jewelry, and other gifts. They deposit these things at the feet of the statue representing that saint. Some even bring animals like cows, goats, or pigs to sacrifice to the spirit(s). After all the sacrifices have been made and the worship is concluded, they go to dance to live bands. Others may also go to the dance even if they didn't sacrifice anything to the demons. They do it as a means of entertainment or taking away stress. Those who go to these festivities most of the time have no clue they are exalting the devil.

For example, in Trou du Nord, on June 23 and 24 of each year people from the local community join with others coming from many other places to celebrate. As a native of the locality, you may go ahead and enjoy festivities like everybody else, thinking it is a party commemorating the birth of the city. Wrong! The whole celebration has nothing to do with the area; they are honoring the demon of that city, who in this case is

"Saint John Baptist," or Jean Dantor. In fact, when cities or suburbs of Haiti are celebrating, they usually state the name of the saint that patronizes that place. For example, they will say, "La sainte Rose (The saint Rose festivity) for the city of Grande Rivière du nord, "La saint Pierre"(Saint Peter's festivity) for the city of Limbé, and so on.

St. Peter is represented in Haitian voodoo by Papa Legba. In voodoo belief, it is said that he holds the keys for both the gates of heaven and the gates of hell. He can take many other forms and operate under different names. For example, he also can be called *Ti Pyè* (Creole), *Ti Pierre,* or *Legba Avadra.* As such, he behaves like a child, a thug, or someone with no place to stay, who wanders a lot. He will cause people trouble by revealing secrets that should have been kept in a family, thus causing them to hate each other. As *Legba Pye kase* (Creole), or "Legba broken leg" (English), he plays the character of an old man destroyed by age. Since he has lost his strength, he comes into the services crawling when he mounts the chwal. Since the majority of the population is Catholic, many feel compelled to attend the services. Under the leading of the church, along with the authorities, all the activities for the saints are organized. People who come to celebrate often bring money to share with the poor and food to feed the hungry. They do so for the sole purpose of acquiring luck. They do not do it out of the love for God or because they care about the people. They were ordered by the voodoo spirits to do this.

At nighttime during the festival, people from everywhere go to the dance. Usually a band or two performs until the next morning. During the night, many things often happen, such as rape, murder, and theft. Many people always report their cars stolen, while others complain about losing their wallets with important documents and money. Young girls, as well as grown women get raped. Some report it, but the majority keeps silent about it because they feel embarrassed and humiliated. Another unfortunate thing that seems to occur every year during the festival commemorating *Sainte Philomène* is that a man has his private part cut off by a prostitute. It is a curse, caused by Philomise/Filomise or Manze Filomise.

There are many people who are both Catholics and vodouisants who go to church only on the day of a particular festival for a saint or saints. Their offerings are not unto God, who gave them health, life, and strength, but to the voodoo spirits. They pretend to reach out to the poor, when in reality their motive is not love. The Lord will not receive their gifts either, for they are filthy and covered with wickedness.

The Catholic Church in Haiti and in the entire world is dragging a huge flock straight to the pits of hell. Many with higher education from major universities are lost in the false teaching of the Catholic Church. When analysts on national television stated that the "pope is infallible," referring to Pope Benedict XVI on his visit to the United States on April 18-20 of 2008, I quickly concluded that, even with higher learning, one can still be ignorant in some respects (referring to the analysts). I respect the pope as a leader. He is a great person who shows strength of character and charisma, but calling him infallible is going overboard. It is like making him equal to God our Creator.

This is what the Roman Catholic Church wants us to believe, that the pope (any pope) has the ability to forgive sins. This is false; it's a lie! Furthermore, the priests, who are lower than the pope hierarchically, also have been given the authority to forgive sins. To this day people go into confession before a priest, and the priest will say to them, "Go, your sins have been forgiven." What a blasphemy it is for a mere human to consider himself equal to God!

Friends, it is only through Christ that your sins can be forgiven. He is the only way to the Father; no other ways or shortcuts were given (John 14:6). Another problem is that the church asks her people to call the priest "Father." Here is what Jesus Himself said concerning this: "And call no man your father upon the earth: for one is your Father, which is in heaven" (Matt. 23:9).

There are many people who claim to cast out demons. Houngans and mambos use some of the rituals of the Catholic Church to expel "bad spirits" from people. Many priests also know how to cast out demons. But are all those who cast out demons doing so in the name of God? And even when they use the Lord's name, are they honoring Him? The answer is no in most cases.

Some are using the Lord's name in vain. Here's how the King of Kings responds to blasphemers: "Not everyone that saith unto me, Lord, Lord, shall enter into the kingdom of heaven; but he that doeth the will of my Father which is in heaven. Many will say to me in that day, Lord, Lord, have we not prophesied in thy name? and in thy name have cast out devils? and in thy name done many wonderful works? And then will I profess unto them, I never knew you: depart from me, ye that work iniquity" (Matt. 7:21-23).

Beware of Appearances

Satan often chooses as his agents people who are kind, who do not look like they could even hurt a fly. They are usually great leaders, though certainly all leaders are not Satan's agents. Because they are in a position of power, they are the best channels through which the devil can mislead mankind. Therefore, you must be careful about appearances. Beware of anyone's seductive ways, their speeches are smooth, and it seems as if you see angels when you see them, but the plans of their hearts are wicked and deceitful.

I can never consider the infallibility of any pope when I know how the papacy throughout the history of the Catholic Church has proved to be imperfect and guilty of crimes, particularly murder. That is why Pope John Paul II had to publicly apologize and ask for forgiveness on March 15, 2000 because of the crimes committed by the Roman Catholic Church. Furthermore, one of the popes, Pope Boniface was known to be so bad that Pope

Clement V had to exhume his body and burn it, as punishment for heresy.

Despite its consistent flaws, the Catholic Church not only has the audacity to make its leaders equal to God, but also to ask that God submit to their imperfect ways. Here is what they say: "God Himself is obliged to be conformed to the judgment of His priest, and one or the other not to forgive or forgive, to agree as they refuse to give the discharge... The word of the priest precedes and God subscribes it."[13]

It is clear that their ways are despicable. Any people who put themselves above God or equal to Him are blaspheming. Do not be deceived!

God is a good God, a jealous Father who does not share His glory with others. You saw what happened to the children of Israel each time they disobeyed the Lord. A journey from the wilderness to the Promised Land that should not take even a month took them forty years. There are no words to describe such a thing as the church coexisting with voodoo. Doubt and confusion will always consume the hearts of those in such a church. Therefore, giving praise to the devil instead of the Lord will seem right to them, but in the end, the devil will torment them in hell because he was never their friend.

You cannot have two masters; Christ Himself said so, not me. If just one of those masters is on the wrong path, you, my friend, will be in big trouble if you refuse to open your eyes. Jesus said, "Let them alone: they be blind leaders of the blind. And if the blind lead the blind, both shall fall into the ditch" (Matt. 15:14).

Over the years, people have been deceived by voodoo spirits. There is no certainty in voodoo; even spirits doubt their own works. When they are going to perform some work, they sometimes say, "We are going to try something and we are hoping that it will work." I don't know about you, but that doesn't sound like confidence to me. How can I trust beings who claim to have power but indeed cannot bring results or lack confidence in themselves.

If voodoo cannot bring comfort and peace, one would think that the church could solve the problem of the people of the land. Not so! We just saw how imperfect and filthy the Catholic Church is and how much it is involved in voodoo. In fact, most voodoo priests and priestesses I have met have told me, "It is safer to sleep in a cemetery than in a Catholic Church." They know how demons control their parishes.

The hope is now resting on the other churches; but are these churches up to the task? I don't think so! Many of the churches in Haiti are dead; they cannot cast demons out of anyone in the church. The power of the Holy Spirit has left them because they have turned the churches into businesses. Most pastors refuse to recognize that they are the problem and they cannot blame everything on the congregation. Yes, the congregation has its part in the body; indeed, without them there wouldn't be a body. But the leaders have the greatest responsibility. They have to set a good standard for the faithful; otherwise the voodoo priests and priestesses will snatch everyone from the church and recruit them for the devil's army.

Many pastors have lost their strength of character by their behavior and the example they set. I know of many young women who have complained about sexual harassment from their pastors. About five years ago, I met a twenty-year-old girl. Her pastor was a friend with her grandmother, so he would come to pay them a visit. He often eats with the family and drinks. But little did they know that man wanted more than just food and drinks. He started making strong sexual advances to the twenty-year-old girl and her little sister, who was only seventeen. They refused him and told their grandmother about the pastor's behavior, but their grandma didn't want to believe them, for she had been a member of his church for a long time.

Under strong obligation, the girls continued to attend church services on a regular basis, but their spirits were not in the church. "Certain times, he would invite us to come and clean the church, but only the two of us and him would be around," explained the girl. "At that point, he would make his move, harassing us. When we could not take it anymore, we left his church and joined another," she added. This happened in Miami, Florida.

Like Voodoo, these churches, whether Catholic or not, are dangerous. You should leave them and ask God the

Father to lead you with His perfect wisdom to the church where His Holy Spirit dwells.

Wherever the Holy Spirit does not dwell that person or place is dead spiritually. People will be living carnal minded because there is no light in them. Their conscious will be lost or blanketed with darkness, which is why fear is able to lodge in their mind and take complete control of them. Things that are wrong will seem right to them. These people are often soaking in religious deception; they love the idea of feeling good without being good. They follow mystery religions and serve the gods of their fathers even after they saw the misfortune due to the choice of their folks. Mystery religion will cause you to fall in debauchery, giving yourselves to pleasure and will give you a freedom that will kill you in the end. Their gods and goddesses are false; their teaching is dangerous. Pray sincerely to God so that you won't be deceived.

My First Communion

I was about ten or eleven years old when I had my first communion. In the Roman Catholic Church tradition, you have to do this, and the church teaches you that Jesus Christ will be inside of you afterwards and you will be able to partake of His body and His blood. However, if you do not take communion, you are a little devil and the Lord will not have anything to do with you; you are a lost cause. I found out this was a lie! Many people today are still falling for it, causing their children to be misled by the devil. They make you believe that if you didn't have a first communion, you cannot partake of the body and blood of Jesus Christ, which blots out your sins. It is done as a means to accept Jesus.

In fact, before you even go that Sunday to the church for the communion ceremony, you must go first to the priest on the previous Friday or Saturday so that you can confess your sins to him in order for him to forgive them. This is to make the children believe that they are too impure to receive Jesus, something that is completely opposite of what the Word of God teaches. The Bible never teaches that you cannot accept Jesus Christ unless you have a pure, sinless heart. On the contrary, Jesus wants you the way you are so that He can cleanse you and present you blameless before the Father. Romans 3: 23 reads, "For all have sinned and fall short of the glory of God and are justified freely by his grace through the redemption that came by Christ Jesus." It is by grace that our sins are forgiven, not by a sinful priest or by our own work. If it is by our work, everyone would go to hell. Therefore, making children believe that they have to have their sins forgiven by a mere man in order to receive Jesus is wrong and one of the biggest lies ever!

To this day people are still being deceived into swallowing this big lie orchestrated by Satan himself through the means of the Roman Catholic Church. Scripture says, "Let no man deceive you with vain words: for because of these things cometh the wrath of God" (Eph. 5:6). As a kid, I really thought the priests had the power to forgive sins, that only they could ask Jesus to forgive me and I could never directly ask the Lord. Seeing a priest was like seeing God face to face in my young mind. But in the meantime, talking to a lwa made me feel as though I saw God too. Spirits had full control of my life, legally because of my birthright. That is why even the day I was supposedly to give my life to Jesus Christ, the lwas had to be involved.

The very Sunday of my first communion, a spirit manifested through my oldest sister came to communicate with me and performed a fire ceremony. I must mention that my sister was taken by the spirits of the underworld at the age of eight. My mom told me that one day my sister went to the river to wash clothes, which was and still is a Haitian tradition due to the scarceness of laundry mats. Suddenly, my sister was nowhere to be found. My mother desperately looked for her daughter, but her search was in vain. Finally, she went home. On her way, she met a man she did not know; he was a voodoo priest. He told her, "Do not be afraid. We have your daughter, and she is safe." Those words were not from the man but from the spirits who mounted him. "That was a relief," my mother explained. Because she was a voodoo believer and practitioner, she was comfortable hearing that.

She received instruction to go back three months later to the same place where my sister was abducted . She did exactly as instructed, and she reported, "When I got to the place, my daughter was sitting on a small chair, holding a handkerchief and a small ringing bell." These things are used in voodoo to invoke evil spirits. "She was speaking an unknown tongue, and when she was speaking the native language (Creole), she was saying things and revealing secrets that regular people wouldn't know," stated my mom. It was clear that the spirits had captured her mind.

It was through this sister that the spirit presented the fire ceremony to me. The spirit lit up a big fire and asked me to cross it at least seven times if I remember correctly. I did so without getting burned. The spirit told me this was for my protection. If I could go through the fire, no one would be able to hurt me. As a result, I felt invincible as a child. I had no idea that this was unpleasing to God, a practice totally contrary to the Word of the Lord, for the Bible says in Deuteronomy 18:10, "There shall not be found among you any one that maketh his son or his daughter to pass through the fire, or that useth divination, or an observer of times, or an enchanter, or a witch."

On the night of that same Sunday, while we were rejoicing, another sister, my mom's second child, was very sick due to a spell cast out on her by voodoo practitioners. As the night went by, her condition worsened. My family attempted to save her life by consulting voodoo doctors, but their efforts were to no avail. Early the following month, she passed away.

It was then that I started to ask my parents why the spirits would let my sister die if they were so powerful. My parents ask the spirits that question for me, and this was how they responded: "We were being blocked by other strong forces so that we couldn't show up to save her." I was a little dubious about that answer, but I accepted it anyway.

Can a voodoo practitioner be also a Christian?

Voodoo contrasts the Biblical Christianity in these ways:

1. Monotheism: Christians believe and worship one God

2. Polytheism: voodoo practitioners believe and worship many gods

3. Worship: Christians worship God in the name of Jesus Christ. Voodoo practitioners worship Erzuli (Virgin Mary), and lwas, etc.

4. Justice: Mercy is the number 1 creed in Christianity. Whereas, revenge is the number 1 creed in Voodoo.

These are just to name a few examples of how Christianity differs from Voodoo. Therefore, it is absurd to say that a voodoo practitioner can be also a Christian. Light and darkness cannot coexist. Sitting in a church doesn't make you a Christian. Being a catholic or a preacher does not make you a Christian either, but a relationship with Christ does. You can profess something but do not possess it. It is an issue of substance over symbolism. Wearing a cross doesn't mean that you have Christ. And doing the sign of the cross is different as having the One who was hung on it. So stop fooling yourself! There is no such thing as Christian/voodoo practitioner. You are one or the other, it's that simple.

Note: There is a spirit behind every toxic tongue, they are quick to curse than to bless you; they will always try to bring you down instead of picking you up. There are those who love to obtrude their nose in someone's business; they are gossips or (gossipy). They also got to find something on somebody and go tell so that they can feel good. These categories of people are often driven by a demonic spirit, ***Legba Avadra***.

Chapter 4
Meet The Virgin Mary

*And I will put enmity between thee and the
woman, and between thy seed and her seed;
it shall bruise thy head, and thou shalt bruise
his heel.*

—Genesis 3:15

Many people I have met and continue to meet are
Catholics and voodoo practitioners who pray to the
Virgin Mary in one form or another (innocently or
willingly). I am also persuaded that millions all over the
world know "Hail Mary" by heart. They still recite it
before going to bed or putting their children to bed.

Besides being the mother of Jesus (the man), who was
or is the Virgin Mary? Religious people have
worshipped her, making her an intercessor for
mankind. Is this biblical? Or is it religion that is luring
people into a false teaching? Was it ever intended for
people to worship her? I will answer these questions
and much more in this chapter. I also advise you to read
this chapter open-mindedly, whether you are Catholic,
Protestant, a voodoo practitioner (that includes every
form of voodoo in every part of the world), atheist, or
agnostic.

Who is the Virgin Mary?

According to the account of Saint Luke, Mary was a
servant of the Lord (Luke 1:38), a virgin (v. 34). The

Lord chose her to give birth to His only begotten Son, Jesus, for a reason that you and I cannot fathom, although we've tried. This is not surprising to a believer, for the Lord's ways are higher than our ways and His thoughts are higher than ours (see Isaiah 55:6–11). An angel was sent to her from God. When he appeared to her, he said: "Hail, thou that art highly favoured, the Lord is with thee"(Luke 1:28). And the angel went on to deliver the news that she would be with child (v. 31). Later on he told her what He (the child) should be named. Mary as a servant of the Lord, without questioning, obeyed the word of God although she was a virgin and engaged to Joseph at the time.

Interestingly, that story, in some religions gave birth to the dogma of "Immaculate conception," which refers to Mary, Jesus' mother, as free of original sin at conception; whereas the "Virgin Birth" would refer to Jesus' birth. This is a distorted view, a belief that has opened the door to many pagan mystery religions around the world and caused many to stray from the truth for centuries. To understand this, we need to analyze the facts and names given to her in some of these religions.

In Haitian voodoo, she is worshiped as Erzulie Dantor, a version of the Catholic Church's Lady of Perpetual Help, and as Erzulie Freda, which has taken on the Catholics' doctrine of the Immaculate Conception. This is called syncretism.

Immaculate Conception: I believe that this dogma has been applied out of context and on purpose. It is one that will lure the children into disobedience, something God strongly disapproves of. According to the definition above, it teaches that Mary was without original sin. Wrong! The Bible is clear (Romans 3:23) that "all have sinned, and come short of the glory of God." Furthermore, in verse 24, we read that we "are justified freely by his grace through the redemption that is in Christ Jesus."

Favor doesn't mean "without sin" as some would interpret it in Luke 1:28 and 30; rather, it is an act by which one receives a gift or anything of value that he or she doesn't deserve. The angel didn't address Mary as "you who are without sin." Instead, the Lord's messenger said, "... you have found favor with God" (vs. 30). Mary and Joseph, just as you and I, were sinners, but Jesus was never conceived with sin. His mother didn't produce the seed; nor did Joseph. God did. Though Mary was a virgin, if Jesus Christ had been produced through Joseph's loins, He would have been a sinner, tainted with the original sin which would disqualify Him as the Savior of the world, the Messiah. So what shall we say then? The seed was pure, untainted, sinless, for God is only good. "Nothing is impossible for Him"; no problem is without solution.

Was it Mary's intention to be worshipped? No. After the angel departed from her, she went to visit Elizabeth who was already with child. She was bearing a son,

John the Baptist. After they spoke to each other and Mary heard what she said, then Mary said:

My soul doth magnify the Lord,

> And my spirit hath rejoiced in God my Saviour.

For he hath regarded the

> *Low estate of his handmaiden:*

For, behold, from henceforth all generations shall call me blessed call me blessed.

For he that is mighty hath done to me great things;

> *And holy is His name.*

And His mercy is on them, that fear Him

> from generation to generation.

He hath shewed strength with His arm;

> He hath scattered the proud in the imagination of their hearts.

He hath put down the mighty from their seats,

> And exalted them of low degree.

He hath filled the hungry with good things;

> And the rich He hath sent empty away.

He hath holpen His servant Israel,

in rememberance of His mercy;

As He spake to our fathers, to Abraham, and to his seed for ever.

(Luke 1:46–55)

In verses 48–49 (shown in italics above) Mary is humbled by the power of God's hand. Contrary to what many believe, she never exalts herself. A few have taken these verses out of context purposely, and they have long succeeded in misleading countless people on the wrong path with false teaching—in fact, ever since AD 431 when the cult (Latin *cultus*, worship) of the Virgin was made official by the Roman Catholic Church at the Council of Ephesus.[14]

Many have openly offered praises and sacrifices to her in the form of Erzulie and many other names in the mystery religions. Some have done so out of ignorance, while others deliberately worshipped her.

Constantine was the man behind all this. He was a professed Christian. However, the truth is he was just a religious politician.[15] He was a worshiper of Tammuz, a sun god. In AD 312, Satan found an opportunity to use him to establish or spread once again his Babylonian religion. Pride set in as two men, Constantine and Maxentius, fought for control of the empire.[16]

Constantine sought help—but not from Jesus. Instead, he called on Tammuz to support him. Satan answered his prayer with a sign that appeared to him in a vision: *"En hoc signo vinces"* (Latin), meaning "In this sign conquer!"[17] When he told people of his vision, they interpreted it in their own way, and soon they started designing various crosses.[18]

Constantine again proceeded after his victory over Maxentius to establish new Catholic churches. His power grew exponentially. Then he gave power to his priests, who successfully converted and recruited the masses. Now instead of having many goddesses, Constantine united the countries under one goddess he called "The Virgin Mary"—at least his own version of Mary: Semiramis, not Mary (Miriam [Hebrew]), the mother of Jesus.

His new religion is a false doctrine that lures people into deception. Before the term "Virgin Mary" or the cult emerged, she used to be worshipped as Diana in Ephesus. Diana is a demon spirit associated with Jezebel. Thus the Mary they now give you through syncretism is a counterfeit one. In Haitian voodoo, she is known as Erzulie Dantor or Erzulie Freda. She is operating under many names around the world, but it is the same face behind different masks. In this segment, I will try to confine myself to the her aspects in Haitian voodoo, while going back in history and the Bible to strip away her mask.

Celebrated on the fifteenth of August every year in Haiti, the Virgin Mary, under the name of "Our Lady of Perpetual Help" or Notre Dame, has become the patron saint of Haiti. Freda, or Immaculate Conception, is celebrated every year on 7–8 December. Erzulie Dantor was the spirit who showed up at the "Cérémonie du Bois Caïman" (14 August 1791). In her form of Isis, she is said to be the friend of slaves and sinners.[19] At the ceremony, Dantor drove a knife into a black pig and had all the slaves who were present drink of its blood. This blood covenant as I mentioned earlier in this book was not only price exacted for freedom but a covenant the people agreed to so that the devil might own the land on a spiritual level. That is why Haiti's fight, more than any other country's, is "not against flesh and blood, but against principalities, against powers ... in high places" (Ephesians 6:12).

As the patron saint of the land, Erzulie (disguised as Mary) is the boss, the goddess who rules over the things of the nation. No wonder why Haiti is the way she is! The Bible says: "Blessed is the nation whose God is the LORD" (Psalm 33:12). The condition of Haiti is deplorable; it clearly and loudly testifies that God is not king over the nation. The nation has sadly embraced other gods and goddesses, with Erzulie as their leader. She is a powerful spirit, and her powers extend over not only Haiti but other nations as well. The book of Revelation speaks of her as the "whore that sitteth upon many waters" (17:1). The angel explained to John, "The waters which thou sawest, where the whore sitteth, are peoples, and multitudes, and nations, and tongues" (vs. 15).

She and her husband Nimrod started the mystery pagan religion in Babylon in the form of Semiramis. They had a son named Tammuz (mother-child cult). Nimrod was the builder of the tower of Babel. When God came down and saw their intention, He confused their language (see Genesis 10:8–10; 11:1–7), and everyone started speaking different languages; no one could understand what the others were saying.

Semiramis is believed to be Nimrod's co builder of the Tower of Babel. She was a prostitute and a very wicked lady. She killed her husband in order to enthrone her child, Tammuz (Little Nimrod), whom she would later marry and kill, as king. Her son Tammuz was not the son of Nimrod. She got pregnant after her husband died. At that moment people started having mixed feelings of her as being now a harlot, now a Virgin Queen.[20]

So she presented Tammuz as Nimrod reincarnate so that people could worship her son as god. In her nefarious mind, if her son was king and worshipped as god, then she was also god or Virgin Mother of god or "Queen of Heaven," also known as Rhea.[21] As Rhea, she was the wife of Kronos who was the father of Zeus.[22] Rhea was also known as "the builder of towers."[23] Keep in mind that all these gods and goddesses are mainly from four people: Nimrod, Shem, Semiramis, and Tammuz.

Ever since Tammuz was a child, she (Semiramis/Isis/Erzulie) viewed herself as totally in control. The child god had to depend on her, in a sense, since she was the ruler. In the illustration below, you can see the way the child is clinging to his mother's arm. This is to depict the child's dependence on the mother. If people need favors, they must go through her if they ever desire their requests to be granted. And the way the mother holds the child shows protection.

The child Tammuz is supposed to be Jesus. Don't you believe it! If you hold this book today, God wants to show you how crafty the world is and wants to show you the truth so that you can be set free. And according to the Holy Scriptures: "If the Son makes you free, you shall be free indeed." As you can see, the emphasis here is on the Son (Jesus Christ) as the Savior, not the mother (Mary/Miriam).

The displaying of the mother-child cult is a hoax; it is a façade. They want to make you feel comfortable worshiping Mary. As Jesus was addressing a crowd, the devil influenced a woman to lift her voice and say this: "Blessed is the womb that bare thee, and the paps which thou hast sucked." Which was a trick aimed at making Jesus exalt Mary. But Christ in His wisdom responded, "Yea rather, blessed are they that hear the word of God and keep it." (Luke 11:27–28).

Whether you are worshipping Mary or a demon masquerading as her, bowing to her is unacceptable, for it is not biblical. What is more, worship given to her son, Tammuz, is detestable and condemned by God. In regard to idolatry, the Lord visited the prophet Ezekiel in a vision and said: "You will see [them doing] things that are even more detestable." The prophet continues: "Then he brought me to the entrance to the north gate of the house of the LORD, and I saw women sitting there, mourning for Tammuz" (Ezekiel 8:13–14).

Haitians, in the voodoo religion, worship Tammuz on 23 June as John the Baptist or Jean Dantor, brother of Erzulie Dantor (Isis/Semiramis).This date was not chosen by Haitians, but it has always been there. In *The Biggest Secret*, David Icke quoted Brian Desborough (*The Great Pyramid Mystery*), who revealed,

The Feast of Tammuz was on June 23rd and celebrated his ascension from the underworld. When he was resurrected, Tammuz was known as Oannes, the fish god, and Oannes is a version of the name, John.[24]

Semiramis was a queen, the most evil queen in Babylon. (The Mary of the Bible was not a queen.) Semiramis was very crafty. She played on the minds of her priests in Babylon by offering them power through flattering words so that they could carry out her evil deeds. They obeyed her and consequently became her eyes and ears in Babylon. She knew almost everything that was going on in the country, thanks to her "holy priests" who informed her of the confessions of the people to them. According to Hislop (1858), this is how the "Confessional booths started popping up around Babylon."[25]

Today, no one can deny the existence of these same booths in our current world of the twenty-first century! As a queen, she delegated to her priests power, influence, and authority which still affect us today. The illustration reveals a crown on her head, but Mary never had one. In fact, at the time of Jesus, the land was under the command of the Romans, so she couldn't possibly be a queen.

The devil is a copycat. He wants to imitate the birth, death, and resurrection of Christ the Messiah. Consequently, he has tried, in many cultures and pagan mystery religions, to promote his version of Jesus and His mother. But he'll never have the real thing. He has used many powerful kings and queens of the earth, but to no avail. For example, Semiramis thought that by copying the virgin birth, she could fulfill the prophecy of Genesis 3:15—the seed or offspring (Jesus) of the woman crushing the serpent's head (i.e., Satan's authority).

Now that same Semiramis/Isis (Babylon/Egypt), Oshun (Cuba), Ashtoreth (Phoenicia and Canaan), Diana (Ephesus) or Erzulie Dantor/Freda in Haiti is not a small demon. She has been around for thousands of years, and her worship has widely spread in the entire world under different names, as we have seen. Every time she took on a name, it meant something. For example, she is seen as the goddess of love in Rome under the name Venus.[26] But her love was not "love" as we know it. Her love brought prostitution to the world.[27] Again, Daniels (2006) reported, "Just like

Semiramis, Aphrodite had many lovers, and temples to her engaged in prostitution and all forms of debauchery"[28] (Note: *Aphrodite* was her name in Greek).

She is a high-ranking fallen angel. Whenever Satan is mentioned, whether as Seth or Lucifer, she (Erzulie) is by his side. In voodoo, witchcraft, or occult practices, as you gain more power and you will meet higher principalities, until you are "worthy" to meet Lucifer face to face. So for her to be exactly where Satan is means exclusive power and authority. Seth was the godly man named Shem who came to Babylon and slew the evil dictator, Nimrod.[29] However, when the pagan religion of Babylon was spread to Egypt, the Egyptians remade the story and presented Shem as the villain in the form of Seth,[30] whereas Nimrod, the villain became the hero in the form of Osiris.[31]

Because of her power and tricks, Erzulie has been successful in drawing many people to her. There are some who worship her innocently; others do so because of what she offers. Those who side with her for the sake of her gifts are the ones who thirst for money and power. She gives them both—but never freely. She loves giving to men especially. Then she will ask them into marriage (see "Marriages in Voodoo" chapter). And when she gets them where she wants them, now they really have to do whatever she requires of them.

In Haitian voodoo, her admirers display her picture in their room, on their altar (*honfour*). Nowadays, now that almost everyone has a cell phone, those who worship her have her picture on the background of their mobile phone. She is even on some people's profile picture on Facebook. If you are Catholic, listen to me: If you really want to serve God, whether you have her picture willingly or innocently in your home, on your phone, in your car, or on your Facebook, I admonish you to take that thing down and burn it. Then find someone, a true Christian, to pray over you so you can be delivered. Worshipping her is idolatry, and Jehovah condemns idolatry. See what happened to the children of Israel because of that! Certainly you wouldn't want to experience the wrath of the Almighty. It is better to obey God than to please any creature and lose your soul in hell.

To the pastors who have her picture in the secret room of their church and to the members of the Protestant church who worship: Yes, I know some of you are her servants. Shame on you. You know better, and you need to repent. And you preacher, you need to close down that church of yours because Jesus Christ is not Lord over it. Your church may be full in attendance, but you are running a dead church. I know some of you have gone to her so your church may increase in number, but I tell you, it is better to have an empty church where Jesus is Lord than have a church where Jezebel and Lucifer rule.

To the ones sitting in the pews but doing the works of the Dantor, God will never hear your prayers. Jesus Christ, the head of the church, affirms, "You cannot have two masters, for you will love one and neglect the other" (Matthew 6:24, paraphrased). If Erzulie is your master, when you pray, even if you mention the name of Jesus, your prayer was in vain. Whatever you call her—Mary, Erzulie, Isis—when you have her in your life, you are doomed! If your intercessor is not Jesus, you're losing the fight; you need to switch sides quickly.

Voodoo practitioners, before they do anything, they recite the Hail Mary either three or seven times accompanied with the Lord's Prayer in the same sequence. Here's the problem. Jesus Christ said, "I am the way, the truth, and the life: no man cometh unto the Father, but by me" (John 14:6). He also said: "...I am the door of the sheep" (John 10:7). And "He that entereth not by the door into the sheepfold, but climbeth up some other way, the same is a thief and a robber" (vs. 1). Many people, priests, prophets, saints, will happily want to lead you to "God" by using their own ladders to reach heaven, but don't be deceived! So it is imperative that we pray to God in Jesus' name and no other. For "Neither is there salvation in any other: for there is none other name under heaven given among men, whereby we must be saved" (Acts 4:12)—not Muhammad, not Buddha, not Allah, and certainly not Mary/Erzulie. What is more, by reciting the Lord's Prayer along with the Hail Mary, one is using God's name in vain, resulting in a direct violation of God's command.

Now that you know the truth, sincerely ask God to give you wisdom, understanding, and discernment so you won't be deceived. The devil is a liar; he is a wolf hiding in sheep's clothing waiting for whom he may devour. "The thief cometh not, but for to steal, and to kill, and to destroy..." (John 10:10). There is nothing more he has to offer. Everything else is a scheme; a marketing advertisement to get you to bite on his deadly bait. Make God your shelter, but the first step is to sincerely invite His Son, Jesus Christ, to come into your heart. At the end of this book, I will show you how to do that according to the prescription of the Holy Bible.

Take the altar call seriously; you don't have time to play around. Do not put anything off for tomorrow. Death can come swiftly, as you have seen with the recent earthquake and other catastrophes around the world. But the train does not stop here. After death, you will spend either eternity in hell or eternity in the presence of Jesus. The choice is yours. I am not trying to scare you, but I am telling you what is true.

Only Jesus Christ can take away your sins. God cannot tolerate sin. He loves us so much that He gave His only Begotten Son for our sake. Christ died for our sins. He does not ask us to exercise logic about it but to believe in our hearts and confess with our mouths that Christ died and was raised from the grave by the Father on the third day. If you deny His sacrifice, you automatically reject salvation; then somebody must die, because the penalty of sin is death. Now that you hear the message, it is your time to get back what the devil has stolen from you. Let's get this beautiful land back that the devil has stolen from us. Come on, this is our time to do right by the only one true God!

Chapter 5
Zombies

See that none render evil for evil unto any man; but ever follow that which is good, both among yourselves, and to all men.

1 Thessalonians 5:15

One of the most atrocious acts in Haitian Voodoo is the zombie phenomenon. These are not the zombies depicted in the Hollywood movies. They are not dead beings coming back to life, seeking revenge, or drinking blood. Nor are they ghosts. They are half-dead people once buried and raised from the grave but with no plain usage of their mind; their spirits are completely controlled by an evil force. Unlike in the movies, where we see dead people walking and become zombies, in Haitian voodoo, zombies are made. How?

Making a zombie is like a scientific project but on a different level. The person is pronounced dead by medical doctors. There are no vital signs; nothing functions. But in reality the person is still alive and can hear everything going on around. The body will be sent to the morgue, but the half-dead will refuse to stay in the ice because of his or her level of consciousness. The morgue's employees out of a good heart can decide to put him or her out of the cold for a few hours of the day, or even the whole time they will spend at the place. If family members of the so-called "dead" are visiting the morgue, they can see the body, or it will be put back in its place. But an employee can decide to let anyone see the body.

We had a friend of the family at the morgue who used to let us see the body when someone was killed through voodoo, just to prove to us that the person is not really dead and to see how evil people can be toward their own brothers and sisters. We used to speak to those half-dead people, and they told us who *killed* them and why.

At that point, they were waiting to become zombies. Waiting, because the person was not yet a zombie until buried and raised through means of evil. I'll explain this later in the chapter.

Many times, our friend invited us to the morgue, and if it was someone we knew, he let us speak with that one. It was terrifying and painful! Imagine knowing that person's family, but you cannot tell them about their loved one, even though they may know that he or she was taken from them through voodoo. If you try to do anything to help the half-dead, you are running the risk of being killed or subjecting those close to you to harm.

Things That Happen at the Funeral and After

The family of the departed is inconsolable as everyone is getting ready to say their final good-bye (so they think). They feel despondent, first, because they know in most cases that their loved one is not actually dead but they are not able to bring him or her back. Second, they know for sure that those presumed dead will suffer harsh punishment after becoming zombies.

The day of the funeral, one person in the family or a friend is usually sent to clean and dress the dead. In their eyes, the person will still be as "dead as Julius Cesar." The body will be then placed in the coffin and transported to the church. The priest or pastor presiding over the service will give his final blessings and comfort those who are in pain because of their loss. During the service, the body is not inside the coffin. The "dead" sits on top of it! Yet no one will be able to see him or her except those with certain power.

After the service they proceed to the burial, but things are not over yet. During the late-night hours, a voodoo priest or someone with knowledge in the field of raising the dead will go and get the person. For the work, the priest usually carries a rope, a whip, and a bottle that contains a liquid unknown to my knowledge.

The Ways Zombies Are Treated

Most of those who are turned into zombies are treated like slaves, if not worse. They are severely beaten, they are raped, the soles of their feet are slashed, and they are subjected to harsh work in big fields day and night without rest. They do not recognize days or dates and have no logic since their minds are controlled by a voodoo priest or priestess. Their bodies can be transformed into any kind of animal except sheep, for they are considered God's animal.

Those who kill someone through voodoo often times go in judgment with his/her victim, after such individual has been brought back to life, but not always. Sometimes they leave the zombie for the voodoo priest or mambo to decide their fate. Once that victim is in the hand of his/her master, that victim will face hardship and hard labors. After using the zombie for hard labor, the owner turns the body into an animal, usually a goat or a cow, and sell it on the market. That animal, which was once human, will be slaughtered at the butcher; then the public will buy it and eat without knowing what they are eating.

Many who are new to the Haitian culture might find this strange, unthinkable, or unreal, but it is a fact. The worst part of all is that the population and the government not only are aware of it, but they also know the location of most voodoo priests and mambos who are killing innocent people and turning them into zombies; yet fear causes them to be silent.

A news report on July 11, 2008 told of a young lady, Ciliane, who had died three years before, who was found in a street of Cap-Haitian. Presumably she had been killed by a houngan named Ti Boss, who used to reside in a suburb called Port Margot. It was after his recent death that the young lady, who was once a zombie, had a chance to get away. The report confirmed that Ciliane testified that she was killed, resurrected, and forced to serve as a slave, working in the field of *bocor* (houngan) Ti Boss, day and night. Reports also said that this voodoo priest was the owner of more than one thousand zombies.

Ciliane was recognized by her family, who took her home. She had two children, a husband, and a mother, whom she saw once again and is currently living with them at a location called Fort Bourgeois near Cap-Haitian. This is real, not fiction. The authorities of the local community and the population are witnesses to the fact.[32]

Crimes of Passion

When we hear about crimes of passion, it is usually about people who brutally murder their partners, mostly because of jealousy, and sometimes kill themselves afterwards. In voodoo, crimes of passion happen are quite different from this. Voodoo practitioners do not kill completely; they turn their lovers into zombies because they don't want to share them. When they are zombies, they can't say no to sex, and the only partners they will have sex with are their masters (boyfriend/girlfriend or husband/wife). I know of at least four people, men and women, who turned their partners into zombies so that only they can enjoy these partners and no one else. But all those who committed these acts have died miserable deaths.

Men who have felt humiliated by women often turn to this crime. I heard of a man who killed a girl because she told him he could never have her. After taking her precious life away, he turned her into a zombie and made her his sex slave. Moreover, my own uncle, my late mom's younger brother, recently killed a woman. After he raised her, he had sex with her and let her husband and family know about his cruel act. He fled the city of Grande Rivière du Nord, where he had committed that crime and took refuge somewhere unknown. Today he is still on the loose.

I believe that everyone who commits such an act should be thrown into prison and kept in solitary confinement with the keys destroyed. There are no words to describe the behavior of those evildoers; their minds are focused only on hurting others, and they bring pain and sorrow to many families.

Zombification of Babies or Infants (Baptized, Unbaptized, or Undedicated)

All voodoo practitioners who own stores and are into making zombies to carry out their own agenda prefer to kill babies, particularly the unbaptized (in the Catholic Church) or undedicated (in other denominations like Protestants) ones. They say there is something special about them; while zombie children are unable to do hard labor, they can be more useful for certain works such as stealing money for their master, or they can be sent to torment your children at night, causing them to have nightmares. That is why those who were raised in the Haitian culture are quick to have their children baptized or dedicated to the Lord.

There are many people who take pleasure in killing infants. Ten years ago, I met a man who said, " I love killing infants, particularly the unbaptized ones. They are perfect to send out to steal money from the major stores of the city." For those of you who are not familiar with the Haitian culture or voodoo, you may think that this was a simple threat or joke. But I can assure you that this is real. Maybe in other societies they are doing something similar through witchcraft or sorcery.

No matter where you are and no matter what form of magic you are exposed to, praying for your children is crucial. Fathers, as the head of the household, it is your duty to bless your little ones. Mothers, if the man refuses to fulfill his duty, take over; protect your children by praying for them constantly, especially at night before they go to bed, so that the loups-garous are not roving around your house tormenting your kids. When you pray, you invite the Holy Spirit of God to take over the house, thus nothing in the world can come near your door and harm your precious ones.

Two Things Zombies Cannot Do

Zombies cannot eat salt, and they cannot look up. Doing either of these things will make them return to normal, something that is unthinkable for a zombie owner. That is why the voodoo priest or whoever is in charge of feeding a zombie will know or be instructed not to give him or her anything with salt. As far as looking up to the sky, I don't know why they are unable to do that. They simply never do it; that's all I know. But the salt, I believe, has something extremely powerful in it. Salt is essential in the life of human beings. We use it in our homes and restaurants because without it some of our food would lack taste. It is also used to preserve meat. In Old Testament times, the children of Israel had to use it when they were offering meats or grain to the Lord: "And every oblation of thy meat offering shalt thou season with salt; neither shalt thou suffer the salt of the covenant of thy God to be lacking from thy meat offering: with all thine offerings thou shalt offer salt" (Lev. 2:13). The New International Version of the Bible says it this way: "Season all your grain offerings with salt. Do not leave the salt of the covenant of your God out of your grain offerings; add salt to all your offerings."

Furthermore, scholars believe that, "salt symbolized hospitality; as an antiseptic, durability, fidelity and purity" *(Smith's Bible Dictionary)*. In addition, salt has life in it; and life with God is eternal. The Scriptures say, "Ought ye not to know that the LORD God of Israel gave the kingdom over Israel to David for ever, even to him and to his sons by a covenant of salt? (2 Chron. 13:5). The word *forever* means "for all time." The one who is King over Israel right now is Jesus Christ, the King of Kings. Jesus is in the lineage of David; sometimes He is even identified as "the Son of David." In Him we have life for eternity and become heirs of the kingdom of God almighty.

I believe it is for all the reasons stated above that zombie owners do not, and cannot, give salt to a zombie.

Sometimes those entrusted to watch over zombies feel compassion and break the houngan's rule by feeding them salty food. The minute zombies taste it, they regain full consciousness; they realize that they are captives, and they run away. At that point, they are called *evade* (French), or "escaped prisoners." If someone who knows them sees them, they can tell their family members, and in most cases the family will take them back, clean them, and care for them.

Some sixteen years ago, there was a lady (zombie) who was found in the street of Grande Rivière du Nord. Her children saw her and claimed her, but the people who had turned her into a zombie came to take her back. The population was outraged, and the affair had to be settled in the local courthouse. The children provided strong evidence that the lady was their mom and that she had actually died. They brought pictures of the funeral, and other witnesses testified in their favor. They also brought pictures of her with the family before she was temporarily transitioned into a zombie. She was fully conscious when they found her, but she was scared of people. She explained all the things she had gone through while she was a zombie. She revealed everything—all the abuse she suffered and who killed her.

The verdict of the court was in the favor of the children. They were given the right to have the woman back. The criminals were sentenced to life in prison if my memory serves me right. The population wanted to have them in order to stone them, but the authorities would not release them.

Other Things Zombies Are Used For

In the countries that are well developed, small businesses, like big industries, all have at least two surveillance cameras. It is a way to protect the businesses from possible burglary and vandalism. In Haiti, things are different. Most businesses have never had surveillance cameras, so they have used zombies to watch over them. Even to this day, those equipped with this technology are still using zombies. If thieves come in to steal, they might be beaten to death. The scary part is that the thieves won't see who is beating them. Even if the thieves do not get knocked out, they won't be able to move; zombies will hold them until the owner of the place shows up. Some business owners will call the police, but usually they deliver the thieves into the hands of the public, who will badly beat them up, and sometimes death will follow.

Zombies also are used to kill people. A houngan or mambo can send zombies to cause someone to get hit by a car, or cause a car to flip over, destroying many lives. Remember, people are unable to see them.

Parallels and Contrasts Between Angels and Zombies

As I said before, the devil is a copycat. The Bible says that in the resurrection we will be as the angels" (Matt. 22:30). In that sense we can do what they do; we will have great strength. Likewise, the devil uses the bodies of the zombies as if they were angels, since they already "face death," if you will. Angels can be visible or invisible; the same is true of zombies. Angels have great strength from God and are willing to serve Him. Zombies also have great strength; theirs comes from the devil, but it is power to destroy. Zombies serve their master unwillingly. Both angels and zombies will accomplish the purpose for which they were sent—angels to "succor and protect man," zombies to kill, steal, and destroy, although unwillingly; in fact, they do not have a will.

Zombies are real! The Haitian government knows it so well that article 249 of the penal code prohibits anyone from turning others into zombies; it is considered premeditated murder and punishable by law. "It shall also be qualified as attempted murder the employment which may be made against any person of substances which, without causing actual death, produce a lethargic coma more or less prolonged. If, after the person had been buried, the act shall be considered murder no matter what result follows."[33]

Whether you are Haitian or not, if you do not have a close relationship with God through His Son Jesus Christ, and you fall under the hands of a voodoo practitioner who kills you, you have a 100 percent chance that he or she will turn you into a zombie. Therefore, whoever you are, do not take the zombie phenomenon lightly; it is serious! Stay as close to God as possible, seek His face, and He will give you refuge under His mighty wings.

Chapter 6
Marriages in Voodoo

Be ye not unequally yoked together with unbelievers: for what fellowship hath righteousness with unrighteousness? And what communion hath light with darkness?

2 Corinthians 6:14

Usually when two people (man and woman) are getting married, they send out invitations to their friends to attend the ceremony. They also make preparations, such as buying rings, selecting music for the special occasion, and deciding what food to serve to the guests. A priest or a pastor is often in charge of the celebration. Blessings will be given by those leaders to the newlyweds, and the groom is invited to kiss the bride. Then they become one as God intended it to be (Gen. 2:24).

It is almost the same process in voodoo, except that the invitations are given by word of mouth only. The voodoo priest or the mambo in charge of the ceremony will not ask the groom to kiss the bride. Why? There is one problem: the person getting married is not marrying another human being but a spirit. A man will likely marry one of the Erzulis. A woman will marry a male spirit. But voodoo practitioners are not limited to marrying only one spirit.

The most ridiculous thing of it all is that most of the time these humans who marry the spirits already have a wife or a husband. The majority of the time, the couple agrees that either the husband or the wife can marry a spirit. There are many who marry spirits in Haitian voodoo. They either do so willingly, or sometimes the spirits tell them, "If you want to prosper or to have protection, take a particular spirit for a spouse."

The Celebration (Marriage)

After everyone is gathered at the place designated for the wedding, the person in charge starts singing. If there are drums available, vodouisants, under the rhythm of such instruments, will invoke the spirits. Everyone present is to participate by either clapping or helping in the songs, dancing, walking in a circle, etc. Usually the spirit getting married will not come until later in the service. There is always a garnished table that is not to be touched by anyone; no food on it is to be eaten unless the spirits manifest themselves and share with people. **The cake cannot be cut** by anyone other than the spirit for which it was made. It will be of particular colors; pink and white cake for example, is for Erzuli Freda.

The person marrying the spirit usually has the ring that only he or she will wear. The spirit doesn't need one, since spirits don't have bodies; they have to possess someone in order to physically attend the ceremony. The weird thing is, sometimes the man as the groom can marry a female spirit that is manifested in another man. Although there is no tongue kissing in voodoo marriages, it is still immoral and awkward for a man to kiss another man on the lips; even though the spirit possessing the man is a female. And it goes the same for a woman; the spirit male she is marrying can possess another woman.

But out of fear, the people end up doing as they are told, thinking that they will be able to protect their assets and their lives or acquire wealth.

The truth is, the devil and all his demons are liars; they are messing with peoples' minds. And unfortunately, there are countless voodoo believers/practitioners who have been deceived. My dear mom was one of the victims of the lies of the devil's fallen angels. A spirit named Sarazin told her she would not die for another forty years. At that time, in 1998, she was fifty-one and terribly sick. I was an eye and ear witness when the spirit made that statement through his "horse" (*chwal*).

Sadly, my mom didn't even see the next month of that same year; she died on May 29 at around 10 p.m., just days after Sarazin made his statement. My late mom, like many practitioners, was married to a spirit, even though she had a husband, my father. It was fine with them, since it is the way of life in the voodoo culture. Her second husband (the spirit), who was supposed to protect her from death, was powerless. Indeed, only God can save you from death.

When you spend all your life denying there is a God, or rejecting Him, all you are doing is making giant steps toward the pit of hell. Most people realize how foolish they were when they are lying on their deathbed, but still they harden their hearts. Yet, some do repent, recognizing that without the Lord, there is no tomorrow. That is why the one philosopher who all his life was an atheist, before dying, affirmed, "If I had to live without God, I should not die without Him." But most voodoo practitioners will not admit that they need God, even in their last breath, because most of them are usually dying in the presence of a houngan or mambo. They will miss going to heaven because they fear the rejection of some spirits, creatures who only make false promises.

As much as I loved my mother, I can't say that she made it to heaven; I am just hoping that she did. I do not know if she ever confessed Jesus Christ as her personal Lord and Savior, and He is the only one who could give her access to the gates of heaven. I truly hope she is there, because I lost the greatest person in my life. But I have great pain wondering if she made it up there!

After the Vodouisants Marry the Spirits

When you marry a spirit, you give that one legal right to your personal life with your human spouse, girlfriend, or spouse-to-be. The spirit can visit you any time. It can even take a human form and come to talk to you; the spirit doesn't need to mount a *serviteur* (see chapter2). There are certain days, mostly Tuesdays and Fridays, when the spirits forbid married people to sleep with their spouses, not even on the same bed. If they violate these days, the consequences that follow will be harsh for both persons on the bed.

A friend of my family by the name of Thorbel had a bad experience with one of the Erzulis. She was his wife, but one day he decided to sleep with his regular girlfriend; that day was Tuesday, a forbidden day for him. That was a long time ago when I was only thirteen, but I remember it just like it was today. This is how he described to us what happened the next morning: "Last night, as I was lying on the bed with my girl, I saw a beautiful white girl with long hair standing next to the bed. I sat up, and she said to me, 'Why are you doing this to me?' And she fell to the ground. Then she said: 'Are you not going to help me up?' I went to get her. As I was trying to lift her up, I broke my back. Her strength was unbelievable for a slim being."

Thorbel was temporarily paralyzed. He spent at least one week maimed in a bed. The spirit was not a natural woman. It might have looked like he was lifting a 115-pound woman, when he was actually trying to lift something that weighed 400 pounds. Spirits can take the shape of anything and make your eyes see something else.

The Danger of Marrying an Unbeliever (Non-Christian)

As you can see in the paragraphs above, it is not safe to enter holy matrimony with just anyone. If you desire to find the perfect spouse, you should lean on God with your whole heart and let Him lead you to the one He chose for you.

Your own eyes can deceive you. Just because you see a beautiful woman who is nice and shy doesn't mean that she is the perfect one. She could be the sweetest person, yet not the one "whose sunshine would warm up your universe." Indeed, she could be a very quarrelsome woman in the house; the spirit she marries can cause her to be bipolar. And it goes the same for a woman who is choosing a man based only on appearances or his material possessions. He could look like Prince Charming and be as rich as Bill Gates, but he would not bring peace and joy to the woman's heart. Money cannot buy love, especially for those who are marrying spirits. Nothing belongs to them. In fact, anything acquired through voodoo will bring sorrow and then vanish away. Beware of whom you are choosing as your mate. That person could be engaged to spirits through marriage! Now that's a real danger!

Don't think that because you are not in Haiti you are safe from this. Right here in the US, there are men and women who come from the Caribbean and are engaged secretly to spirits; and even some who were born here are in the same boat. Although voodoo is more developed and concentrated in Haiti, evil spirits in general are everywhere.

Many are those who vowed to voodoo lwas and have traveled throughout the world. Countless numbers are residing in the US, Canada, and France. By migrating to these lands, they have made it easy for the spirits to use them as vessels spread their deception to more people.

Thus, taking any man or woman with that particular engagement with the devil for a spouse is like throwing yourself into the lions' den. That is probably why a great thinker once said this concerning marriage: "Marriage is a funeral in which the man is able to smell his own flowers." The harmony, if there is one in the union, is not given by God but by the devil. He was given a legal authority to rule over the couple's intimacy because of one of them. Remember, in marriage you become one. Therefore, both must be pure before the Lord. He does not take part in darkness and impurity.

Your body belongs to your spouse in marriage, but through the counterfeit doctrine of voodoo "marriage," your body belongs to a spirit. That is why the spirit can set up days for you to worship him and not sleep with your spouse or lover. In that case marriage is simply, "Yesterday we made love on the sofa; today I'm sleeping on the sofa." You end up doing the will of the devil instead of the will of God. Life in the house has no direction because the Word of the Lord is not the final authority in the family. Demons will invade the house because one is married to a spirit. You can have a house, but you need the Lord's presence to make it a home.

Marriage is certainly a beautiful thing, but Satan and his agents have defiled it. Government officials have passed laws that support same-sex marriages; this is an abomination. The Bible says, "Whoso findeth a wife findeth a good thing, and obtaineth favour of the LORD" (Prov. 18:22). Notice that God is not talking about same sex here. "He" represents *man*; he is not to find another man but a woman. When Jehovah God brings the special one into your life, it is favor because a good spouse is hard to find, especially in these last days, when immorality and impurity have consumed the heart of the world.

Because of the moral decline of society, many people have rejected the idea of getting married. Women don't choose based on quality but on reputation—good or bad. Men choose a woman only because of her outward beauty, forgetting completely that the exterior of the package doesn't say anything about the gift. I read about a seventy-five-year-old single woman who vowed to stay celibate. When asked why she doesn't need a husband, she replied, "I have a stove that smokes, a parrot that curses, and a cat that comes home late." Most men who practice voodoo do not respect and cherish their wives. And most women who practice voodoo do not submit to their husbands as they should. The fear of God among them is nonexistent.

Married Against Their Will

There are people who are hypnotized because of a spell and make decision they would not have made if fully conscious. But I want to talk about those who are married without their awareness.

This is something that happens mostly to male *serviteurs,* or servitors (those through whom spirits are manifested). If such a man refuses to marry the woman a particular spirit approves of, he will be forced to marry her, or he will find himself married to her. I know a man who married his wife without his knowledge. Although the lwas told him to choose her, he refused. After much pressure, he finally accepted, but against his will. On the day of the wedding, he was tending his field, taking care of his garden. Everyone was waiting desperately at the church, but there was no sign of him. All of a sudden, he appeared; but there was a problem: his body was there, but a lwa had mounted him. The priest proceeded and married them, with the spirit acting as if he was the man. At the reception, the spirit left man. Little did he know, he had been married.

He was dressed like a farmer before the spirit mounted him, but at the reception he was wearing a suit. Since he is a *serviteur*, he knew that he had been possessed, but in the eyes of the public, he was the one who vowed to take the lady for his wife in the good times and the bad.

Could a couple like that be happy? Absolutely not. The love of God is not in this union. God did not choose them to be together; the spirit did. In reality, they are not even married, because there was no agreement between them. The spirit through him said yes, but he did not. Thus, she is in reality living as his concubine. Because of fear of the lwas, he could not divorce her; he had to stay with her against his will. They had children before marriage and lived together, but the intention of the man was not to get married. There were times the couple wouldn't talk to each other for months. The only time he would communicate with her was when the spirit mounted him, or when the spirit gave specific orders for him to do so.

You must choose a mate wisely, whether you are dating or planning on getting married. Your partner could be deeply involved in voodoo, the occult, or other witchcraft activities. People who embrace these ungodly practices become arrogant and proud, for the devil and his demons control their hearts, causing them to have a bitter attitude. People like that are disrespectful toward their mates in the house and in public; they think they know everything. There is no healthy communication at all among them. I heard about a couple who didn't talk to each other for weeks. Everything they wanted to say to each other was done by writing. One day, the man was supposed to attend an important meeting, so the preceding night he handed a note to his wife that read, "Wake me up tomorrow morning at five." When he woke up the next morning, it was 10 a.m. He was infuriated and started cursing. But as he looked on the lamp table next to his bed, he saw a note that his wife left him that read, "Wake up; it's five!" Bad communication can break a good relationship.

Voodoo is not a good basis for happiness in marriage, especially for those who are married to a lwa. There is no divorce from the voodoo spirits. Voodoo practitioners can't bring the spirits to court, because they are not human. Even if they were able to do so, fear would paralyze their thinking. All in all, they are stuck for life, unless they break the engagement with Satan's acolytes by the power of the blood of Jesus Christ. If you are reading this book today and you are married to voodoo spirits but can't get out because you are plagued by fear, know that God loves you and promised to deliver you from all of your troubles.

The government making Voodoo a national religion is a dangerous move to the people of the land. Doing so is directly dedicating Haiti once again to Satan. What is more, as a religion, marriage that is supposed to be sacred, will be conducted by Voodoo priests/priestesses. They will be given authority to celebrate the union between a man and a woman. This is unbelievable what these people are doing to Haiti! Where are going with this generation? Marriage will be much more defiled. People will be married out of fear, because if a *hougan* tells a voodoo practitioner to get married, he/she will much likely do so, for they know what the consequences could be if they do not honor the command of the such voodoo priest. Open your eyes people! Marriage is a lifetime commitment, you should carefully choose your mate and do not rush it. God do not recognize the authority of any Voodoo leader, therefore, your marriage is invalid before the Lord. God did not join this union, but Satan through his priest did. Consequently, there will always be chaos and quarrel in the house. Without the love of God, the house will still be a house, not a home. A family needs a home, somewhere things are peaceful, positive and permeating with the love of God. It is a joy to come home and fully persuaded that everything is all right. But if Satan is the master over that place, destruction, confusion will reign.

Chapter 7
Who Is Satan?

Be sober, be vigilant; because your adversary the devil, as a roaring lion, walketh about, seeking whom he may devour.

1 Peter 5:8

The Caribbean, and particularly Haiti, has what are called *loups-garous*. A loup-garou (man-wolf or were-wolf) is a person possessed by an evil spirit, who gets up at night to prey on people in the streets. Their targets are primarily children and all those who travel during the night. They usually take the shape of animals, such as dogs, cats, donkeys, horses, or chickens; they even take the shape of tigers or lions although these wild animals are not native to Haiti. Many of those who have become **loups-garous** did not ask for such a curse. They consulting voodoo priests too much, and the priests got tired of their presence and cursed them with an evil spirit that causes them to hunt people via sorcery. Just as the devil cannot stand the light, neither can the *loups-garous*; they have to go back to their home before daylight. This is no fiction! Even today there are many people who are possessed by these evil spirits. Their objective is to cause fear and kill.

People's lives in Haiti have always been engulfed by deep anxiety about black magic (voodoo) and crime. There are always reports of loup-garou activities, especially in the suburbs. Many of them have been beaten to death if they get caught. It is not easy to stop them, but in voodoo there are levels of power; there are those who simply find pleasure in stopping the loups-garous in a mystical way, just to make money off of them. Once trapped, they have to pay whatever their captors ask for or they will be kept there until morning. They often do their best to comply with the demands, because if they get caught while daylight is approaching, the population will murder them.

I knew a man by the name of Moscou, who is now dead. His only satisfaction was to get up at night—I mean every night—just to stop those "men-wolves" and keep them captives if they did not pay him. He had some strange power. Everyone in the local community knew him either by name or by face or both. He used to be called "the guardian of the community." He would walk great distances, like a foot patrol for everyone close to him so that he could protect them from these evildoers. Did he do this by the power of God? Absolutely not! Satan's kingdom is divided within itself. The pride among them is tearing them apart. If someone has more power than another, he or she will try to demonstrate his or her abilities by trying to hurt the other. Many have committed horrible crimes because of greed caused by pride. The crafty one is behind every bad thing; it is his nature to raise people against one another.

In my career as a police officer in Haiti, I worked on many cases that brought tears to my eyes and pained my heart. From larceny to murder—I have seen it all. I was working in the southeast region (Port A Piment), when one day someone came to complain about two young men who had just murdered their parents. I have to mention that the police in Haiti, in that particular area, did not have easy ways of communication and transportation. In order to report a crime that occurred even two miles away, somebody had to walk to the police department and inform us. But that crime had happened some twenty miles away. We had one Toyota vehicle for fifty-two officers, so only four of us went to make the arrest.

When we got to the place, the public showed the assailants to us. We questioned them, and they confessed to the crime. Here is their confession: "We had an argument with our mother and father over a piece of land that we had asked them for. When they refused to give it to us, we took a machete and cut our father in pieces and buried him. Then the following week, we did the same thing to our mother." This was horrifying and there are no words to explain these acts. They were found guilty and charged with first-degree murder. They are still serving time in prison. Selfishness and ambition caused them to act this way. The Bible puts it like this: "For where envying and strife is, there is confusion and every evil work" (James 3:16).

On another occasion, this time was in the north region (Grande Rivière du Nord), I was on patrol with two other colleagues, Marcelin and Joseph, when we noticed people running. A lady waved her hands, signaling us to stop, so we did. She said, "A group of *chanpwel* (just like loups-garous but more evil and more powerful; they are often associated with the word *sosyete,* or *society,* hence *sosyete chanpwel* to designate them as a group or society) met with another group that had only kids. The adults captured them in order to carry them to secret places, where later on they will sacrifice those kids, eat their flesh, and offer their blood to the gods."

I sped to the place, and when we got there, some of them fled the scene. We arrested four of the adults and brought some of the kids who were hurt to the local hospital, because some of them had been badly beaten.

The devil has his grip so hard on the people of that land that even their kids are exposed to evil practices. There is no peace among devil worshipers; two groups honoring the same gods want to kill each other. They are rooted so deep in voodoo that they are blinded by the veil of ignorance. In 2 Corinthians 4:3-4 we read, "But if our gospel be hid, it is hid to them that are lost: in whom the god of this world hath blinded the minds of them which believe not, lest the light of the glorious gospel of Christ, who is the image of God, should shine into them."

Satan Is the Father of All Lies

John 8:44 says, "You are of your father the devil, and the desires of your father you want to do. He was a murderer from the beginning, and does not stand in the truth, because there is no truth in him. When he speaks a lie, he speaks from his own resources, for he is a liar and the father of it." This is an attribute that no one wants to have I'm sure. We all know how much it hurts when someone lies to us. There are lies that can even cause death. Lies have caused wars that resulted in all kinds of loss, pain, suffering, and sorrow. Hitler killed 6 million Jews in the Holocaust. He lied about them by labeling them *Welt fiend* (German), or "world enemy." Because of the untrue things said about the Jews, many unfortunate events have occurred in their lives. The Crusades, for example, were military campaigns of the Roman Catholic Church to gain control of Jerusalem from the Muslims and to punish the Jews as the alleged "Christ killers." What is more, the crusaders set fire to the synagogue and listened to helpless women, men, and innocent children screaming in horror, begging for mercy, as they were burned alive. And the crusaders marched around the synagogue, singing "Christ, we adore thee" while 969 people were cremated.[34]

Lies can also cause families to be dissolved. One member of the family with a bad lying habit can make a household a living hell, and this is exactly how Satan wants things to be. He always creates confusion because he never wants us to be happy.

Satan Is a Tempter

The devil tried to tempt Jesus with wealth and power. "Again the devil took Him up on an exceedingly high mountain, and showed Him all the kingdoms of the world and their glory. And he said to Him, 'All these things I will give You if You will fall down and worship me" (Matt. 4:8-9). The devil will show you goods that are not even his; then he will ask you to deny God's Word. The Creator, on the other hand, gives principles rather than conditions. His love is unconditional. He loves us no matter what we have done. After Adam and Eve sinned, God could have said it's over. But instead He felt compassion and showed us His mercy by sending His son to die for our Sin: "For God so loved the world that He gave His only begotten son, that whoever believes in Him should not perish but have everlasting life" (John 3:16).

The devil is so tricky that, he will even use the Scripture to prove his point. The Bible says, "And he [Satan] said to Him, 'If You are the son of God, throw yourself down. For it is written: "He shall give His angels charge over You. And, In their hands they shall bear You up, lest you dash your foot against a stone"'" (Matt. 4:6). If Jesus didn't have the knowledge of the Scripture, He would have easily fallen for that seduction. But our Lord, the King of Kings knew the devil's scheme and replied, "It is written again, 'You shall not tempt the Lord your God.'" (v. 7).

Satan uses power and money to entice us. It is sad that many are falling right into his trap. But the truth is, Satan doesn't own anything; he is a thief. Be careful!

Someone said, "Power is the ability to bring results." But whose power you use will determine what kind of result you'll have. Do not ignore the fact that the enemy is powerful, but in Jesus Christ you are more powerful than he is (1 John 4:4). God is all-powerful (omnipotent), all-knowing (omniscient), and everywhere present (omnipresent). From whom are you seeking answers, from the liar (the devil) or from the Provider (God)?

Unfortunately, many people have turned to the devil for answers because of pride and impatience. In pride they want to be on top of the world so that they can humiliate and abuse others. Those people who use the stairs of ignorance to throw their dirt on those at the bottom are nothing but fools. When they boast about their level of achievement, it is only to make others feel low. Even when they are doing their duty, it is only to make themselves appear superior to others. Their road to so-called prosperity is paved with hatred and deception. What does God's living Word says about pride? It is written, "For I say, through the grace given into me, to every man that is among you, not to think of himself more highly than he ought to think" (Rom. 11:3).

Impatience is also a factor that causes certain people to turn away from God. They let the devil come and tell them, "He has nothing to do with you. Worship me, and I'll give you what you need now." Sadly, they take matters into their own hands, trying vainly to change their future by listening to Satan. They do not realize that the same thing that seems like a blessing to them also can be a curse. I heard about my eleventh-grade math teacher and his friend, who were tired of their financial conditions. Instead of seeking the Creator, they went to a voodoo priest, hoping that he would give them luck so that they could win the *borlette* (a mini-lottery in Haiti). But the houngan gave them a fatal liquid to use on their body. He told them that at night the winning numbers would be revealed to them in their dreams. They went to sleep, excited that the next morning everything would be all right and they would never have to work again, because the agent of the devil had guaranteed they would win. Unfortunately, they did not even see the next day. They died the same night. Everyone who knew them was saddened by their sudden death. Their impatience and greed killed them.

Satan Is a Destroyer

Destroy comes from the Latin *destruere*, meaning "to undo." When God created man, He created them in His own image and breathed life into them (Gen. 1:27). But the devil came and ruined their lives and brought death to all mankind. The devil led them to believe that they would not die. His words proved to be a lie. His goal was to supersede God, to place himself higher than the Creator. His attempt was unsuccessful, and the angels of the Lord drove him and his accomplices out of heaven. Thus, he is out to avenge his fall by attacking the Lord's most precious creature, us humans. This fierce adversary is serious and determined.

The book of Job is a most compelling story, and it reveals the determination of the evil one (see Job 1:8-11). Job was a sincere and honest man. He feared the

Lord and always did what was right. But the devil chose to destroy him. The enemy will never stop; his attacks are dangerous, brutal, and cruel. In one day Job lost all his material possessions and his children (Job 1:13-19).

Today the devil is still after our souls, the very thing the Father loves the most. Satan is trying to find souls to join him in hell. He is using all sorts of tools to mislead mankind: power, money, and anything immoral. He already knows his fate and that he cannot ward it off. So he is miserable because of what he knows, but like the saying, "misery likes company," the adversary doesn't like solitude.

He Is the Enemy

An enemy is someone who wants to destroy you; he is opposed to your success and your progress. The deceiver is always on the offensive. He wants to bring you down at all costs. He wants to lead you to a place so deserted in your life that the only water within your reach is the tear running down your cheek. He wants to turn your friends and family against you, making you feel so lonely so that you will curse God and give up on all of your dreams.

The evil one wants his word to supersede God's. He likes to create hostility in a peaceful environment and raise confusion. He presents himself as a friend, but it's only appearance. We read in 2 Corinthians 11:14 that "Satan himself masquerades as an angel of light." The truth is, he has no light in him; he is the darkness itself.

There are many in today's society who display Satan's characteristics. They are sweet talkers who want you to believe that they will be there for you, when, in fact, there is nothing but deception in their hearts, hidden under a flattering attitude. A friend will tell you what is wrong with you, comfort you, and help you to be on the right path; he will expose your flaws so that you can correct them and be a better person. A foe will manipulate you, seduce you, and take all you have and leave you hanging when you need him. In contrast, a friend grieves with you over your losses and intercedes for you in prayer.

Sometimes we get hooked up with the wrong crowd and refuse to realize that they are enemies who will cause our destruction. God determines who walks into our lives, but it's up to us to decide whom we will let go. Many times we think that our success depends on others instead of on the Almighty, and when they fail us, we are disappointed. Satan will always want you to be stuck with the people who lock you in the cage of their own opinions. He wants his agents to be your friends so that they can cause you to do his will instead of the Father's. The devil wants to separate you from the Creator, and separation from God is death. Satan is and always will be the enemy.

He Is an Accuser

Satan will always remind you of what you have done wrong in your life so that he can make you feel sorry for yourself and cause you to eternally live in fear. Imagine him as a prosecutor. He has all the charges against you, with strong, fully documented evidence to prove your guilt, and he is ready to condemn you. In your mind, it seems impossible for you to get out of your mess because you are aware of your wrongdoings. Everything is exposed, and your conscience is tearing you apart; a tornado of remorse is ravaging your heart.

I have great news for you! While you are grieving over your past and thinking of how to handle your defense, a mighty lawyer is rushing down from heaven, faster than light, to come to your rescue and plead your case. He says, "Yes, I do not deny the charges against my client. Everything the prosecutor is saying is true. But there's one thing, Your Honor; two thousand years ago, I laid down my life for this client. I shed my blood to purchase his life, and no matter what he has done, he was pronounced righteous before this court. As You have set this precedent; his sins are never to be remembered against him." And the great Judge, God almighty, declares judgment in your favor. You are not only set free but also granted eternal life!

From the Devil's Mouth to God's Loving Arms

In this section I present the powerful testimony of a young girl who fell under the grip of Satan but was rescued by the power of the Holy Spirit. This is the testimony of a very brilliant young girl, now twenty years old, who went to hell and came back. Five years ago, Scindy Albert faced her greatest fear. This is her testimony about that shocking experience.

It was a Friday, and I was at home with my little sister, I was bored; everything annoyed me. All of a sudden, a friend of mine, a Chinese dude, came to the house and asked me if I wanted to smoke with him. I said yes. I was so bad at that time that I even asked my little sister to join us, but thank God she refused! Minutes after I took some puffs of crack and cocaine, I felt like my head was heavy; so I lay down on the couch. Suddenly, I saw something standing in front of me. I was scared. I jumped up and started running from it, for I felt that it was the spirit of death coming to get me. As I was running, I was screaming: "I am going to die! I am going to die!" What I feared happened! I died and immediately went to hell. As I stood there, a man wearing a white dress was standing in front of me. He started telling me all the things I have done wrong. Everything came back to me, and I felt guilt and remorse running down my soul. I said, "But I am virgin; I don't belong in this place." I thought that being a virgin could save me, but I was wrong. The man said, "You belong here because of your wrongdoings." After saying that, he disappeared.

As I stood by myself, transfixed with fear, I could hear other people screaming in pain, but I couldn't see them; they were paying the price for their own deeds. I felt like I was burning, but there wasn't actually a fire. My body was twitching. I felt horrible; the place was unpleasant. Everything was moving and happening extremely fast. I said to myself, "I don't want to be here for the rest of my life." But there was nowhere to run or hide.

As I was looking around, I saw in the distance turning objects moving faster than a helicopter blade. In my mind, they were like doors, and I felt like I had to go through them. But something told me that if I went through the wrong door, I would be there forever. Fortunately, a very powerful force guided me through the right one. Although I was not a Christian at that time, I could tell that this was the Holy Spirit of God. Once I ran through the right door, I was back on earth. I found myself by the Chinese dude and my little sister. I told them frantically that I was in hell, and I asked them how long I had been gone. They told me that I just passed out for approximately five minutes; but to me it felt like a month, for the many things I endured couldn't possibly have happened in only five minutes.

When I went back to earth, I wanted to see my mom very badly. She was doing laundry near our house, about three minutes' walk away. It took me about fifteen minutes to get to her because my steps were heavy and it was painful for me to even walk. My mother was shocked at hearing what had happened to me and was saddened to see me in pain.

That deadly experience brought me to the point of depression. I became schizophrenic for a while, and I had to be admitted to a hospital. At every moment, I could hear people talking in my head, telling me that I am nothing. Voices have told me to cut myself, and I did as they told me. When I was hospitalized, if I heard other people talking, I felt that they were speaking against me, and I got aggravated. I had to be on medication to fight my depression because it was to the point that it could have destroyed my life.

Despite all my troubles, I decided to quit my medications and get the right antidote for my toxic emotion, Jesus. I gave my life to Him. But at first I did it because I wanted protection, not out of a sincere heart. As time progressed, I truly came to understand salvation and really devoted my life to Jesus Christ as my personal Lord and Savior. For the first time in my life, I experienced peace; and the joy that invaded my heart was beyond comparison.

Today Scindy is on fire for Jesus. She is a strong woman of God. When the devil accused her, Christ redeemed her by the power of His blood. Know this: you can never go so far that God is not able to save you. He has a plan for each and every one of us. Maybe you are doing something bad in your life right now. Before it gets too far, turn around and invite Jesus into your life. He will change you and make you whole, for He promised that!

Chapter 8
Angels And Demons

For I am persuaded, that neither death, nor life, nor angels, nor principalities, nor powers, nor things present, nor things to come, nor height, nor depth, nor any other creature, shall be able to separate us from the love of God, which is in Christ Jesus our Lord.

Romans 8:38-39

The word *angel* means "messengers"; angels are agents of God. An agent is someone with a particular power who represents another, whether in business or government. An FBI agent (Federal Bureau of Investigation), for example, has the power to investigate high levels of crime for the US government. The agent can arrest people who commit felonies, such as terrorists, money launderers, spies, and traitors. Police officers are also agents of a government. Their mission is "to protect and serve." They are striving day and night to get the bad guys off the streets. Here in the US, where violence has escalated considerably, they have been given power by the justice system to arrest with or without a warrant. They can arrest without a warrant in cases such as when the criminal is caught committing the crime (flagrant) or when there is "probable cause."

We also have the CIA (Central Intelligence Agency), which is "a U.S. federal bureau responsible for intelligence and counterintelligence activities outside the United States." In addition, there are the US secret service agents whose jobs include the protection of the president of the United States and his family.

Then there are the border patrol agents and US customs agents, who make sure our borders are secure; they prevent or reduce illegal entries or reentries to the land. By doing so, they represent a major part in the government because they help fight terrorism along with the other agencies. These are just a few of the government agencies or agents, and their duties are not simply limited to what I have described.

While a government agent protects the land and the people and the Constitution of the United States of America, a business agent works for the well-being of a company. A real estate agent, for example, in most cases will have a good relationship with clients because they need each other.

As agents of God, angels are assigned by Him to guard us here on earth (Ps. 91:11). We read in Psalm 34:7 that "The angel of the Lord encampeth round about them that fear him, and delivereth them." Scholars have noted that the expression "the angel of the Lord" is used for the presence of God Himself. Genesis 32 recounts how Jacob met with the angel of the Lord and wrestled with him for a whole night and prevailed (v. 28). In verse 30 we read, "And Jacob called the name of the place *Peniel*: for I have seen God face to face, and my life is preserved." I know people will find this controversial when reading that verse because the Scriptures also say that "no one has seen God." But you need to understand that the ways of God are beyond human comprehension. He is omnipotent; nothing is impossible to Him or too big for Him to do; beyond that it is useless to speculate on His nature, for He is unfathomable.

Angels are beautiful and brilliant in appearance. Considering the fact that they have been assigned to protect man, they have, without doubt, great strength. God would not have delegated that role to them if He did not equip them with power. They also will fight against and destroy those who oppose God and His children in the final days: "And the first went, and poured out his vial upon the earth; and there fell a noisome and grievous sore upon the men which had the mark of the beast, and upon them which worshipped his image" (Rev. 16:2).

Angels are ministering spirits. Jesus our Savior was ministered to by an angel when He was praying on the Mount of Olives before His arrest and crucifixion. As His time drew near, He felt sorrow and was anguished, but "an angel unto him from heaven, strengthening him" (Luke 22:43). Not only do they minister to Christ, but they also minister to us as well. The Holy Bible says, "Are they not all ministering spirits, sent forth to minister for them who shall be heirs of salvation?" (Heb. 1:14).

The angels are innumerable. When the Roman soldiers came to arrest Jesus, one of the disciples drew his sword and cut off the ear of the high priest's servant (Matt. 26:51). The way Christ responded to that action not only confirmed the strength of the angels, but also leads us to realize how difficult it is for us to even guess their number. Here is what the Lord said: "Thinkest thou that I cannot now pray to my Father, and he shall presently give me more than twelve legions of angels? (Matt. 26:53). It is impossible to say how many legions of angels there are; nor can we say how many each legion has. They are, like the stars, countless.

Moreover, angels are holy. They worship God day and night; they are constantly in Jehovah's presence. A day will come when we redeemed humans will be with the Father, but not in these impure bodies. We will be given new bodies, like those of the angels; and at that point we will not be under the weight of death, for sin will exist no more.

In any government or business, there is a *hierarchy*. It is the same in the angelic realm. The archangels are more powerful than the regular angels. The archangel Michael, for example, has outstanding power. In fact, he has been assigned on his own to protect man against stronger demons and Lucifer himself. He drove the adversary and his subjects "out of heaven" when they waged war with God (Rev. 12:7-9). There are also the cherubim and the seraphim, who are considered the highest ranking in hierarchy of all the categories of angels. The cherubim are the ones assigned to guard the gates of heaven. "So [He] drove out the man; and [He] placed at the east of the garden of Eden cherubim, and a flaming sword which turned every way, to keep the way of the tree of life" (Gen. 3:24). They are also depicted on top of the ark of the covenant (see Exod. 25:18-19), they are four-faced creatures: man, ox, lion and eagle (Ezek. 1:10). Some scholars believe that their quadruple face signifies wisdom and intelligence (man), strength (ox), kingly authority (lion), and swiftness or farsightedness (eagle).

Although all angels are spirits, not all spirits are angels. As you have read before, one quality of angels, who offer unceasing worship to the Almighty, is holiness. Lucifer was an angel, and holy, until the day he let pride invade his heart and deceive him. Since then he and his acolytes are labeled as "fallen angels." The adversary became the Prince of Darkness. He is the ruler of demons and is in fact a "demon" himself.

When Jesus was casting out demons, the Pharisees doubted that His power came from God. They accused Him of casting out demons in the name of "Beelzebub." Jesus then answered, "And if Satan cast out Satan, he is divided against himself; how shall then his kingdom stand?" (Matt. 12:26). Satan's kingdom is as divided as the Shiites and Sunnis, who are always fighting each other; the only time they will get along is when they are planning on killing Americans, Jews, and Christians. Demons are the same in the sense of oppressing and tormenting the innocent, and they are united in their efforts to recruit souls to join them in hell.

In these last days, the adversary and his defeated warriors are forever on the offense. Just look at the news. The events occurring in our world today testify of the wickedness of the Evil One. Chaos is enveloping the world. In early 2008 in Myanmar, bizarre weather claimed the lives of over 62,000 people and left about 2 million without shelter, food, and clothing, CBN (Christian Broadcasting Network) news reported on the *700 Club* show on May 29, 2008. The same source reported that in China a violent earthquake killed over 80,000 people and left thousands homeless.

In recent years, killer storms, tornadoes, and tsunamis have devastated properties, destroying lives and infrastructures and leaving many homeless and governments powerless. Hurricane Katrina until this day maims New Orleans. Many were forced to leave their homes and start all over again because they lost everything they had worked hard for. That is why Christian ministries like Breakthrough and the 700 Club's Operation Blessing, along with Christians around the world, put their hearts close to those that are suffering losses of any kind, by extending their hands of love to help those in need. By doing so, they are showing the love of Jesus Christ through the help they provide in clothing the naked, providing shelter for the homeless, reaching out to the poor, giving medical attention to the sick, and feeding the hungry.

Friends, God is glorified each time we display love for one another, for it is the "greatest commandment." Love creates an atmosphere of unity and peace that pride, jealousy, and fear cannot overcome. Whenever the devil is destroying, God is restoring, and it is usually through us that He reaches out to ones in need. He is a Father who will "never leave you nor forsake you"; He will extend His hand of love and rebuild whatever the enemy had eradicated.

After a natural disaster strikes, many people ask why a loving God would allow such a thing to happen. Let me tell you that He has nothing to do with anything bad. When hurricanes and tsunamis and floods ravage a land, people always blame the Creator. But God never broke His covenant with man. He is too faithful to be unjust. Remember, in the time of Noah, when the ways of man were not pleasing to the Father, Jehovah gave Noah instruction to build an ark to save him and his family from the coming flood, along with all who were willing to change their ways and listen to the voice of the Lord. But the people hardened their hearts, and they were destroyed by the flood. They turned their eyes the other way and continued in their wickedness, and they paid with their lives. God promised Noah and his sons that He would never erase man from the earth by a flood: "And I will establish my covenant with you, neither shall all flesh be cut off any more by the waters of a flood; neither shall there anymore be a flood to destroy the earth" (Gen 9:11).

Man has created devices that can annihilate the entire world, and some people of this world, under demonic influences, are willing to use them against their fellow humans. The world has become an undesirable place to live. Take, for example, the former president of Iran, Mahmoud Ahmadinejad, who promised to "wipe Israel off the map." One can quickly conclude that this man had some demons controlling his mind, paralyzing his ability to think straight. The scary thing is that he was/is working expeditiously to acquire nuclear weapons in order to accomplish his goal. He faces one problem though: "He who watches over Israel will never slumber nor sleep" (Ps. 121:4). Therefore, it will be impossible for him and his allies to see their objectives come to pass. Still they remain a menace to the rest of the world. Jesus warns us of the way things will be in the last days: "And ye shall hear of wars and rumors of wars: see that ye be not troubled: for all these things must come to pass, but the end is not yet. For nation shall rise against nation, and kingdom against kingdom: and there shall be famines, and pestilences, and earthquakes, in divers places. All these are the beginning of sorrows" (Matt. 24:6-8).

Humanity has endured two world wars in the past century. Today rumors of war captivate people's minds as the **red horse and rider** of Revelation 6 are making huge stride, making their footsteps heard. Words like *terrorist threat, terrorist attack, Al-Qaida, Hezbollah, and Hamas* have caused people to be transfixed with fear of flying or of frequenting crowded places. Neighboring countries refuse to live at peace with each other. As I write, the presidential election in the US is drawing near, and the economy and the Iraq war, Afghanistan and North Korea threat are the hot topics on the news. Gas prices have reached a level we never seen before in the States, food prices are higher, and salaries remain the same.

These conditions have outraged the people living in the United States. If it so in the richest country on planet earth, how much worse is it then for countries like Haiti and various places in Africa or South America? The famine is so intense in Haiti that the citizens of the land have labeled it "Clorox," to describe its harshness. Children there and around the world have died in large numbers because of starvation. Many of our little ones have died because of hunger. The few who survived are heroes who, despite the odds, managed to keep focus in school. Even for us as grown-ups, when we are starving, we temporarily suffer from abulia. To make matters worse, the devastating earthquake of January 12, 2010 left over 250,000 dead—over 1 million homeless (see my book: CAN GOD SAVE HAITI?), and countless in makeshift tent cities cramming into every open space in Port au Prince. I went there in September 2011 I left shell-shocked and depressed; but still keeping hope alive that one day soon, the condition of my beloved people will change.

You need to understand that there is a demon behind everything bad: poverty, misery, murder, idolatry, lies, adultery, sickness etc. Demons are real, Jesus Christ knew so. In fact, He cast them out of many who were possessed and oppressed. He healed a woman crippled by demons for eighteen years (Luke 13:11-13). He healed the boy suffering from seizures caused by a demon (Matt.17:14, 18). While Jesus knew demons are real, they had full knowledge about Him being the Son of God. After He had calmed the storm and got off the boat, He confronted two demon-possessed men, and they said to Him, "What have we to do with thee, Jesus, thou Son of God? art thou come hither to torment us before the time?" (Matt. 8:29). They knew the power of Christ came from the ultimate source; in fact, He is the source. Before He went to be with the Father, Jesus gave His disciples peace and left among them the power of the Holy Spirit (John 20:22). To this day, those of us who are in Christ have the same power within us.

Today as the surge of Holy Spirit power is more and more present, a rise in the occult, sorcery, witchcraft, and voodoo is also being vividly manifested. In Haitian voodoo and around the world, necromancers are performing their acts of calling up the dead for answers. Mostly they call on dead saints and family members who have passed away. They are said to have "familiar spirits," something condemned by the Scriptures. The Bible warns us of "spirits of demons performing miraculous signs." And in Leviticus 19:31 the warning is clearer than the day: "Regard not them that have familiar spirits, neither seek after wizards, to be defiled by them: I am the LORD your God."

Communicating with the dead is very popular in Haiti. In most households, when someone dies, the family usually consults a voodoo priest or mambo to invoke the deceased in order to find out who killed him/her. If the person was killed by means of spells, a demon masquerading as that person will appear to the family members and tell them who the killer(s) was, and revenge will eventually follow. They will invoke the spirit of the alleged killer, who will appear before them in a mirror. With a knife given to them by a voodoo priest, they will stab whoever passes in the mirror. If the person dies in the object, so it will be in his or her actual life. That's one of the reasons why there are so many sudden and mysterious deaths in Haiti.

Some call on the dead for advice and guidance. By doing so, they are violating God's law and putting their lives at risk. The Bible says, "And the soul that turneth after such as have familiar spirits, and after wizards . . . I will even set my face against that soul, and will cut him off from among his people" (Lev. 20:6).

The embracing of demons in a society leads to rampant immorality and perversion. Furthermore, demons can lock you up in a cage of generational curses, from which only the blood of Jesus by the cross can set you free and make you whole again. In Haiti, those who are not under the blood of Jesus Christ are slaves to voodoo and its demons. I know of a lady who lost four children, and each time one died, her gods said, "It was a mistake; this won't happen again," until all of them passed away. She believed the word of the evil spirits and continues to serve them even after she has been deceived.

The eyes and minds of those who are worshiping voodoo spirits are veiled; they are blinded by this generational curse. Even though they never find

154

answers that satisfy their needs and bring them peace, they are still hooked on voodoo. Of them the Bible says, "Now the Spirit speaketh expressly , that in the latter times some shall depart from the faith, giving heed to seducing spirits, and doctrines of devils" (1 Tim. 4:1).

The activities some people have undertaken have allowed demons to enter into their lives. If you steal one time and then become a recidivist, whether rebuked or not, you can bet a demon spirit is controlling that area of your life. Every rapist, murderer, and child abuser has a demon behind him or her. Loups-garous, or "men-wolves," are controlled by demon spirits. All those who cast spells on others to destroy their lives by cursing them are doing so with the power of demonic forces.

In Haiti, demonic activities are why many people become crazy or are handicapped. If the spirits hate you and cannot kill you, they will make you lose the plain usage of your mind or cripple you for life. Demons are as real as they were in the time of Jesus Christ. Remember the story I mentioned earlier of the woman who was crippled because of demons. Today the demons are even more serious about their quest for human souls because they know that their time is at hand.

In the US children are being exposed to demonic spirits through books such as *Harry Potter* and other books about witchcraft. Moreover, TV programs like *Buffy the Vampire Slayer, Angels,* and *Charm* provide more exposure for both adults and children to the occult. Music, which should be comforting, has become a source for promoting violence, depending on the kind you and your children listen to.

Not only are the children exposed to the occult, but they are also not safe from violence or crime. "On Tuesday, April 20, 1999 at Columbine High School, two students Eric Harris and Dylan Klebold, went on a killing spree in Jefferson County, Colorado and murdered 12 other students and a teacher, 23 were also injured, then the perpetrators killed themselves. It is the fourth-deadliest school killing in United States history."[35]

More recently, on April 16, 2007, at Blacksburg, Virginia, two separate attacks were made on Virginia Polytechnic Institute and State University (Virginia Tech), with approximately a two-hour interval. The assailant, a young South Korean-born student, Seung-Hui Cho, killed thirty-two people and wounded many others before committing suicide. News reports further added that "it is not just the deadliest school shooting, but the deadliest shooting rampage by a single gunman in U.S. history."[36]

One can quickly conclude that these young men were driven by demons. The devils want to convince you in your mind that the bad is good and you should just go and act upon your emotions. However in doing so, you will lose your life and your soul for eternity. I don't know why these guys would murder so many people in cold blood. What were they going through? No matter what it was, I am certain they didn't let "the peace of God that surpasses all understanding" dwell in them. Instead, they let the devil lead them either to follow their emotions into vengeance or to commit these horrible, premeditated crimes just for the fun of it. The sovereign Lord says, "To me belongeth vengeance and recompence; their foot shall slide in due time: for the day of their calamity is at hand, and the things that shall come upon them make haste" (Deut. 32:35).

Demons are always out to torment you and make you feel worthless. They will tell you that you are a reject, that society doesn't need you, and that you can't amount to anything. Demons provoke situations in your life that can later develop into depression. They will even cause you to hurt yourself or others. Your life will be as if it has no meaning. You may want to get out of your conditions, but you just won't seem to be able to.

Well, don't lose hope, for "greater is He that is in you than He that is in the world" (1 John 4:4). The power that raised Jesus from the grave is inside of you if you are a Christian. If you have allowed demons to enter into your life or the lives of your children, you need to rebuke them by the blood of Jesus. Don't be ashamed of using the name of Christ; there is great power in it. Demons tremble at the mention of the name of the King of Kings and submit to it.

Ask people who believe strongly in the Word of God and practice it to pray for you. Don't make friends with demons; cast them out of your life as soon as you feel their presence. If you find yourself thinking or doing something that is not in accord with the Word of the Lord, you are under demonic attacks; come against them immediately with the power of blood of Christ.

The devil is not playing around; he's attacking God's children all the time. You certainly cannot sit around and ignore the power you have in the name of Jesus. Use it, for it is beneficial for you and others. "Our job is to empty hell and fill up heaven," said a fellow Christian. God does not bless us so that we can be selfish; He does it so that we can be a blessing to others. If you have a gift in healing, pray for people who are sick. It is not always about you, but about others. In fact, as Christians, it is our duty to pray for others and a mandate to cast out demons.

Chapter 9
Fear, the Devil's Weapon

Be strong and of a good courage; be not afraid, neither be thou dismayed: for the Lord thy God is with thee whithersoever thou goest.

Joshua 1:9

One dictionary defines *weapon* as "a device to inflict injury or death on an opponent." Years ago people used weapons like spears, bows and arrows, and swords. David used a sling to kill Goliath, and later it became a weapon of choice for Israel's army. Second Kings 3:25 reads, "And they beat down cities, and on every good piece of land cast every man his stone, and filled it; and they stopped all the wells of water, and felled all the good trees: only in Kirharaseth left they the stones thereof; howbeit the slingers went about it, and smote it."

Today, great armies of the world have weapons of mass destruction. Some even have nuclear weapons or are on the verge of acquiring them. Although there is peace talk on earth, people around the world are aware of the imminent threats of those who oppose democracy and justice, and certainly they represent a great danger to the world. But the sovereign Lord says that, "He will destroy those who destroy the earth" (Rev. 11:18). Satan, along with the people he has misled to destroy the earth, will also be put into the lake of fire and cut off from the face of the earth forever.

Are the weapons mentioned above the greatest of all? I doubt so. Even though nuclear weapons can erase the world, I would not say that they are the most powerful weapons of all; the most powerful weapon is *fear*. Fear was, is, and will always be the devil's weapon of choice. Satan can use your fear against you and divert you from doing the will of God.

We are fighting the most powerful enemy anyone can fight. The Bible says, "For we wrestle not against flesh and blood, but against principalities, against powers, against the rulers of the darkness of this world, against spiritual wickedness in high places" (Eph. 6:12). This is why the devil doesn't want you to pray. He knows that prayer means power. He often brings doubts to overwhelm your heart and cause fear, which will confuse your thinking. The reason most Christians don't see results from their prayers most of the time is simply because they pray with their mouths but don't believe in their hearts. Then, they will let the enemy drag them to a place of deception.

Fear is what prevents you from moving forward. Do not let the adversary lie to you, saying that you will never amount to anything, that God is not going to answer your prayer. He will feed you with false promises, saying that he can give you a nice car, a nice house, or a better future. But how can he offer something of value when his own future is so bleak. His future awaits him in the pits of hell. I believe this is something you do not have to share with him!

To have a better *future*, you must let God take full control over your:

Finances

Uncertainties

Troubles

Upsets

Relationships

Emotions

Your Future

Finances. Most people are working and still struggling to make ends meet. Their jobs provide them with a paycheck that is not even enough to pay their bills. Working is a great thing, of course, but you don't need a job to succeed. Instead, you need to work smartly. Along with that, you need to bring your tithes and offerings into the house of the Lord. That will trigger the blessing of the Most High in your life. The devil will not dare touch your blessing. In fact, he will even have to repay seven times what he has stolen from you. Tithing is the only area in which God asks people to test Him. Malachi 3:10 reads, "Bring the whole tithe into the storehouse, that there may be food in my house. Test me in this, says the Lord Almighty, and see if I will not throw open the blessing that you will not have room enough for it." When we don't pay our tithes and offerings, God says in His Word that we are robbing Him (Mal. 3:8). Today, there are many of you who are wearing stolen jewelry, driving stolen cars, and living in stolen homes. You may think that you made it on your own, but the Bible says, "But thou shalt remember the Lord thy God: for it is he that giveth thee power to get wealth, that he may establish his covenant which he sware unto thy fathers, as it is this day" (Deut. 8:18 KJV). If you take Him out of the picture, you become a thief, and destruction is awaiting you on your path.

Uncertainties. Are you uncertain about your future? Don't be! A wise man once said, " I may not know what my future holds, but I know who holds my future." When you accept Jesus, the Scriptures say you become a "new creature." All your sins are forgiven by the power of the blood of Christ. Furthermore, you become an heir of the Kingdom of God. Can you imagine becoming an heir of everything that Bill Gates owns? Wow! You would feel like the richest man on earth. What Bill Gates possesses is not even a dot compared to what the Father owns. The Bible says, "The earth is the Lord's and the fullness thereof" (Ps. 24:1). Wow! Now that's what I call a true heritage and riches. Not only will you share everything with Christ, but you are also guaranteed the gift of eternal life through salvation by the blood of the lamb, and all of this is free. Do not let the enemy still your joy by bringing fear, which creates uncertainties. God always honors His promises.

It is by worrying too much that we became uncertain. Worry is toxic! It can cause you to die while you are still living. It will make you afraid to make decisions because you are not sure if you will succeed. For example, worrying about what people might say might keep you from going back to school as an adult. Don't worry. Dessalines, the "father of the independence of Haiti," learned how to read when he was forty. Some years ago, I was watching the *700 Club,* and I saw a news report on an old man, ninety years old to be exact, who graduated from high school, alongside many young teenagers. Stop being lazy; God is not tired of you! If you acknowledge Him, He will stretch out His mighty hand and reach out to you. Stop listening to the voice that keeps on telling you cannot. Listen instead to the voice of the Holy Spirit, who says, "You can do all things through Christ who strengthens you."

Troubles. "I have learned, in whatsoever state I am, therewith to be content" (Phil. 4:11). You may not like your present situation. All the weight of the world may seem to have dropped onto your back. Such things as health issues and financial hardship can cause you to be discouraged. Just remember that God will never leave you. He may allow your current situation to take place in order to shape your life and prepare you to do His work. With fear, Satan poisons your mind, bringing you trouble, but the Lord uses your troubles as an opportunity to promote you if you keep the right attitude.

Take Joseph, for example. His brothers sold him into slavery because they were jealous of him. He was falsely accused of rape by Potiphar's wife and thrown into prison. Most of us do not have it as bad as he did, but through all his troubles, Joseph stayed faithful to God by continuing to live his life straight before the Lord. He spent over a decade in slavery, but God took him from the prison and promoted him to the palace as the second most powerful man on the face of the earth. His attitude toward his problems was positive, although his situations were unpleasant. Thanks to his obedience and his humility, he saved a whole generation from famine because he did not have any resentment toward those who had hurt him and he forgave them.

Upsets. The reason most people get upset is that they put their trust in people more than they do in God. If a sudden change (negative) occurs unexpectedly in their lives, they are disappointed. In such cases, you need to call on the Father for help; your hope should be in Him only. Here on earth, when you call somebody too often asking for favors, they will get away from you or change their phone numbers. But the Lord wants you to dial His number, because it is a telephone of unconditional love that always rings and is never busy.

God wants to know that you depend on Him for all your needs, just as a child depends on his or her father. A father feels happy when his son comes to him and says,

"Dad, I need your help." He has great pleasure in this and feels like a king, knowing that the child is depending on him for support. Likewise, God our Father in heaven is delighted to know that we acknowledge Him and that we admit we cannot make it on our own.

Relationships. The Bible says, "In all thy ways acknowledge him (the LORD), and he shall direct thy paths" (Prov. 3:6). Most of the time people make decisions on their own, particularly when it comes to relationships.

Marriage is a lifetime commitment; therefore you need to choose a spouse wisely. Let God direct your paths toward the person of His choice and vice versa. You certainly would not want to share a home with someone who makes the house a living hell. To choose somebody based on your emotions is a mistake you don't want to commit. Imagine marrying someone who is engaged to evil spirits (see chapter 5). You can forget about a healthy union. All you will encounter is turmoil and torment. Because of the choices they make, many people have created cavities in their relationships that later they will fill with pains and regrets.

Emotions. People from all walks of life have let their emotions prevail in one way or another when it comes to decision making. Your emotions can get you into trouble. Most the time when we rely on them, we find ourselves fighting God's will. When we are being too emotional, we are letting our soul make the decision instead of letting our inner being (spirit) tap into the power of the Holy Spirit. When your soul is in conflict with your spirit, confusion starts kicking in. This happens when we are not in alignment with the Spirit of the Lord. Consequently, our physical body starts making wrong choices, and sins become evident. Jesus knows this, and this is why He told His disciples, "Watch and pray, that ye enter not into temptation: the spirit indeed is willing, but the flesh is weak" (Matt. 26:41). Our bodies require certain things, including clothes. But we often want to look better than anyone else and boast about how much we spend on clothing. Life is not only about those things of the world, however. The spiritual things are of much greater value.

Another thing we need to avoid is getting bitter and negative all the time. If something doesn't go your way, continue to put your trust in God and let Him direct your steps. You may be seriously in debt, but the Lord shall provide for all of your needs (Phil. 4:19). Your health may be challenged today, but know that "by His stripes you are healed" (1 Pet. 2:24). Do not live your life on emotions, for the heart is deceitful and most decisions come from it. Let the Spirit of God guide you; that is a sure guarantee that you will not fail. A bright future is what we all hope for, but without Jesus Christ, you can say good-bye to your future. You don't have one!

In a sermon at my church on the first Sunday of June 2008, my pastor, reverend Richard Séjour, talked about something very intriguing. Concerning the future and afterwards, he raised a question: "If you could live 120 or 200 years, would you trade eternal life for that?" he asked. The whole congregation was quiet like a tomb. Everyone was looking at their neighbors, and in their eyes I could tell that none of them wanted to go to hell. They would not trade eternal peace for eternal torment. They would not miss the eternal appointment with the Lord, Jesus Christ and enjoying the wonders of heaven that God reserves for those who love Him. The Bible says, "...Eye hath not seen, nor ear heard, neither have entered into the heart of man, the things which God hath prepared for them that love him" (1 Cor. 2:9).

The Fear of Rejection and Voodoo

For every a piece of land, or *abitasyon* (Creole), owned by a Haitian family, there is a master for that land. That master is the spirit who claimed this particular family through the ancestors. Usually family members go to their *abitasyon* to find answers to their problems by invoking that spirit or presenting gifts and/or sacrifices to him or her. Sometimes the spirits take the shape of a human or animal and come to talk to them, or sometimes the spirits speak to them in their dreams. On the flip side, if the people of the family abandon that place, the belief is that their lives will be miserable until they return to it.

There many voodoo practitioners around the world who go back to Haiti every year to their *abitasyon* to offer sacrifices to the lwa who occupies that piece of land. However, if one year they fail to do that, it is considered rejection, and they can lose everything they have worked hard for. Fearing that the spirits will ruin their lives, they feel obliged to make sacrifices in order not to displease the lwa.

Houngans and mambos, in particular, are extremely afraid of rejecting their lwas. They should be, if they do so with their own strength and not Jesus Christ. I know of many voodoo priests/priestesses who have died because they refused to serve their lwas. Yes, they renounced the spirits, but they never entered into covenant with God through His Son. Instead, they played it neutral and paid with their lives.

There are also those whose parents are strongly involved in voodoo. But as they are growing up, they hear the Word of God and realize that the practice of voodoo is not for them. They want out but, their parents won't let them. In many families, the parents threaten to disown their children or kill them if they abandon voodoo. Some of these young adults let fear of rejection choke them, and they have died and lost their souls. Yet others come to the Lord and grow in faith in Jesus Christ.

Friends, you need to understand that your parents are not always right and one day you will have to face judgment. They won't be there for you, and they cannot write your name in the Book of Life. I agree you should listen to the instructions of your parents, honor them, and love them. But you simply cannot afford to let them put you in a path that leads straight to hell. It is better that they disown, for God will embrace you because you chose the right way.

Rejecting the devil and his acolytes is absolutely the right thing to do, but you need to look for protection. If you do not, Satan will kill you; and when you are in hell with him, he will torment you day and night. The only solution is to be covered by the blood of Jesus Christ, for that is the only way by which you can be under God's protection. Then the lwas, the demons in hell, and Lucifer himself can't harm you. However, don't think everything will be like milk and honey. The devil will always persecute you, but he will not win the battle. He will attempt to get your soul, but Jehovah will not let that happen.

Don't be surprised or panicked when those attacks are coming your way because you have rejected the devil. Jesus, the Son of God, had to go through a series of temptations from the enemy, which He resisted. Furthermore, He suffered great tribulations because of the sins of humanity. He was falsely accused, beaten, spit upon, mocked, and shamefully crucified. But through all these pains and sufferings, He stayed obedient to the Father for the sake of you and me. Today that same Jesus, who conquered hell by defeating Satan on the cross, is knocking at the door of your heart wanting to give you His peace. Would you open up and accept Him? This is His promise for those who obey: "Behold, I stand at the door, and knock: if any man hear my voice, and open the door, I will come in to him, and will sup with him, and he with me. To him that overcometh will I grant to sit with me in my throne, even as I also overcame, and am set down with my Father in his throne" (Rev. 3:20-21).

Voidness

When something is void, it has no value. For example, a check that is void is useless. There might be money in the account of the person giving it to another, but the recipient of a void check cannot withdraw those funds. *Void* also can be used in the sense of privation, emptiness, or pointlessness. Thus, while fear is the devil's greatest weapon, voidness is the most powerful ammunition in his arsenal. With fear, the enemy creates a void inside of you, making you feel less than nothing. He will cause you to live your life without purpose. You will end up doing a bunch of things that have no meaning because you don't have a goal or all you are doing is trying to please others. You will lose your sense of originality by trying to be somebody else. The devil creates this emptiness in you so that you can depend on him. He tells you to follow him, but in the end his road will lead to eternal destruction.

This is exactly what happened to the people of Haiti. The vodouisants have a void that they think only voodoo is able to fill. As I explained in chapter 2, voodoo practitioners, houngans, and mambos all live in fear of each other; and the Bible is clear concerning the fear of man: "The fear of man bringeth a snare: but whoso putteth his trust in the LORD shall be safe" (Prov. 29:25). That is why voodoo is so wrong, because when you fear another human being, you actually call death upon yourself; that person or creature you fear will control almost every aspect of your life.

If you let the fear of voodoo control you, you will be miserable. Think about it; if here on earth, the devil and his troops are creating a tornado of troubles, torments, and confusions in your life, what makes you think things will be better in hell? On the other hand, God wants you to enjoy life right here and right now; then when you go to your final destination—heaven—you will find joy and peace that words can't even describe. With God, you have the best of both worlds. With Satan, you have the worst of both worlds; your sorrows never end.

If you find yourself trapped in voodoo, witchcraft, the occult, or any types of wicked practices because of fear, know that there is a God who cares for you and promises to help you. The same God who created this perfect universe, with everything well balanced and controlled by Him, is longing for you to turn away from evil and acknowledge Him. He will not force you; it's a decision you have to make on your own. Keep this in mind; the very earth where you are right now was once void and formless. The beautiful scenery, the rivers, the ocean, the birds, and you all were created by the hand of the Almighty. "In the beginning God created the heaven and the earth. And the earth was without form, and void; and darkness was upon the face of the deep. And the spirit of God moved upon the face of the waters" (Gen. 1:1-2).

If a God like that can create such a wonder out of something formless and empty, surely He can fill your heart with great things. In fact, you are a wonder, but the devil doesn't want you to know or believe that. For this reason, he takes the Word of the Lord out of you quickly and fills you with his words. Don't be a fool! Do not be deceived. If you hear the Word, do not harden your hearts. I will say again, voodoo is worthless. Don't waste your time in it. Instead, come to Christ, and you will experience joy like never before. Learn this from one who was once a voodoo practitioner.

You may say, well, "I was born in it, I can't just let my parents down." I understand your fear, but in the end it will be between you and God, your priest, parents, pastor or your friends and other family members won't be there with you in judgment. You will answer God for everything you've said or done with the knowledge you had of the truth. You must be set free, you can no longer be a slave of voodoo; you were created in the image of God, refuse to be called a horse. God said, "You are fearfully and wonderfully made" (Ps 139:14), don't let the enemy turn you into a worthless creature without purpose. Honor God! IF you're dealing with that native "birthright" know that I've been there and I can help you.

Native Birthright

In this segment, I will talk only briefly about some of my experiences in voodoo. I actually grew up in a voodoo family. My mom, dad, brothers, and sisters were all involved in this practice. As a child, I pretty much didn't have a choice, and I always thought that voodoo was from God since the Catholic Church is also involved in most, if not all, of the rituals (see chapter 3). I was blinded by fear and ignorance. Of course I could not understand certain things in my younger years. But, in addition, my parents did not have the true knowledge to guide me in the right direction for they themselves also had grown up in the fear of voodoo. This is what I call native birthright.

Take, for example, a child born into a wealthy home. All that his parents have, or a part of it, he will inherit one day. But while growing up, he will enjoy the wealth, and his parents will train him to acquire more and to save what is legally his for his children and so on. The same is true for someone who is raised in voodoo. Parents who are voodoo practitioners dedicate their children to the spirits. Even the names of most of the children are given by a lwa. Thus, a legal authority was given to the gods to control the lives of these children and manipulate them. It is the devil's way of keeping the nation under subjection to him so as to cause the people to perish. As the children grow to old ages, they in turn will train their descendants to do exactly the same.

As a child, I always thought that voodoo was my strength and my refuge. This mentality stayed with me for years. I thought the lwas were God's angels sent to earth to protect Haiti. I could not see anything wrong with the practice of voodoo, because my parents went to church every Sunday and forced me to go. I have to admit that I did not enjoy going to church. All I learned was "Our Father in heaven" and "Hail Mary," which is exactly what a voodoo priest or priestess does before invoking the spirits. Because of that, I strongly believed that they were working for God; therefore, whatever they had my parents to do for me, I had to accept.

My parents never questioned the voodoo priest when he said they were to give me and my brothers and sisters *special showers.* I was told that these were for protection; if someone wanted to do evil to us, he or she would not succeed. But I always felt a strange feeling after those showers. They were nothing but a bunch of leaves and some water, cologne, perfume, and powders, which mixed up together gave a very unpleasant smell. I often wanted to refuse taking those baths, but I was powerless against my mother especially. Furthermore, it was unthinkable for me to tell them I didn't want that, because the lwas led them to believe that it was for my own good.

My Struggle with Attacks from My Sister's Murderers

Some weeks after my sister's funeral, I began to feel symptoms of headaches, which later developed into fever. My mom consulted a medical doctor, but no problem was found. Yet my health became worse. My father was away from home because of his job. He was a corporal in the Haitian military at that time, and he was in an isolated environment. A voodoo priest was quickly consulted. He concluded that I have been exposed to a spell. He added that the same people who killed my sister through magic wanted me dead also. Everybody was shocked because I was an innocent kid.

One day around noon, I was lying down, and my older brother was also on the same bed, when the sorcerers sent three zombies to take me alive. They were only in the form of skeletons, two by my feet and one holding my head, trying to lift me up. My brother seemed to be in a deep sleep, even though he was not normally a sound sleeper. In fact, he couldn't have been sleeping since he had just lain down on the bed; apparently they had made him incapable of knowing or seeing what was going on. I turned around to try to shake him, but my hands could not reach him. I felt like I was maimed. I was transfixed with fear. At that time only one thing was in my head: to call upon God. I said, "Oh God, don't let them take me like they have done to my sister!" The moment I said that, they disappeared and my brother jumped up.

I went straight to my mother who was in another room, where we had a little grocery store. I explained to her what had happened. Immediately she said, "We can't stay here. We're going to see your uncle." My uncle lived in a place called Desdune, a suburb in the department of Artibonite. From our home in Cap-Haitian, it was a good three hours in public transportation and then a walk on foot of at least five miles to get to Desdune. That place is highly known for voodoo doctors who are very evil in their practices. My uncle knew most of well-known houngans and mambos.

We got there in the middle of the night, my mother, my older brother, and me. Early the next morning, my uncle brought us to the a voodoo priest. I wouldn't remember his face if I saw him today, but I remember that he was a very scary-looking guy. He put us in a room, where he invoked a demon. All we heard was a loud and strange voice asking us, "What are you here for?" Only my mom answered, saying "I come to seek deliverance for my son." That's all I remember hearing. After their conversation, the spirit directed my mom to the voodoo priest, who told her and my brother what to buy in order to start on my treatment.

They did everything they were asked to do. The witch doctor sacrificed animals and prepared some shower with different kinds of leaves, powder, and other things—I didn't even know what they were. Still, I did not get better; instead, I got worse. They took me somewhere else—same scenario. And every one of these places required money, nonrefundable of course.

Though I called upon God when I was afraid the zombies would kidnap me, I was still unable to decide for myself, since I was just but a kid about eleven years of age. Therefore, whatever my family decided had to take place. Next, they took me farther west to a small city called Grand Goâve, not far from Port-au-Prince, the capital city. We did not stay in the heart of Grand Goave but went to a remote location in that area. This time my oldest sister was with us. That voodoo priest was well known in this area for healing people and killing people; he was vile. His attempts also were worthless.

Desperate to find a solution, my mom and sister headed back north with me to a man well known for his voodoo power. His name is Jacques, and he's from a place called Marmelade, the same place the former Haitian President, Rene Garcia Préval, is from. Going to this location was the last resort, because almost everyone in Haiti, as well as Haitians overseas (US, Canada, France, and other places), respects this voodoo priest to a point that some even worship him. He can invoke demonic spirits to quickly kill, to heal those that were cursed through evildoing, and to help people to get money in some mysterious ways. Every year, those that were engaged with the demons manifested in this man brought gifts and sacrificed animals and even human lives in order to get their lives spared by the devil. Despite his power, he was unable to treat me; all his works were idle.

While I was over in Marmelade, I had a strange dream. I saw my dead sister come to me dressed in a red robe. She started chasing me, telling me, "I came to get you." In the dream, I saw that I was in my house in Cap-Haitian. As she was running after me in the dream, I saw that she broke many things in the house. Then all of a sudden, I woke up. I was petrified. I quickly explained the dream to my parents, and they were panicked as well. Later that same day, we went back to Cap- Haitian, the drive was at least two and a half hours. When we got home, everything was messed up, with broken glasses everywhere; nothing was in order, just as I saw in the dream. I was even more frightened then.

Two days later, the sorcerers who wanted me dead sent a dog to my house, which hid under my bed. Keep in mind that in the voodoo realm a dog is not what it seems to be. I think I was in my mother's room when two friends of the family frantically yelled, "Where is that big dog coming from?" They knew we didn't own any pets. It was a huge dog, so they used bats, rocks, and magic to kill the unnatural creature. Thank God, I was not in my bed that day! The dog was so heavy that four strong men couldn't even carry it. They called for more help in the neighborhood, and threw it into the ocean. I was still sick by the way.

After many failed attempts to find a cure for my unknown condition, my family finally found a man named Sarazin with a quiet personality but who served a powerful spirit. He performed his tasks, and in three days I was healed.

Sarazin was adopted by my parents as part of our family. In fact, my mother had me call him "godfather." He maintained a close relation with me for years. He gave me a shirt that someone had bought for him, a multicolored one, and a bottle with a special liquid. These were for me to use in case I had a feeling that something was wrong, even if just a light headache. I was to use that bottle or put on the shirt when I felt afraid. At night, because I was afraid of the loups-garous, I put the shirt on and used the liquid like cologne. I wore it when I was going out, particularly if I thought I would be facing danger. I destroyed those articles (in 2006) a year after I became a Christian in 2005. I went back to Haiti, threw them away, and prayed in the room. I refused to let the demons find a means to be where I live.

Chapter 10
Breaking the Chains

Greater is he that is in you, than he that is in the world.

1 John 4:4

In your family life, you must be a chain breaker. You must be the catalyst that brings change into your life and your family. This cannot be any truer than in breaking the chain of voodoo liaison in your life. Remember the devil comes but to kill, still and destroy (John 10:10). It doesn't matter how *well* you serve him, sooner or later you will get killed and curses will follow your family line because of you. Maybe that curse or curses have followed you because of your Mom and/or Dad but you can change and I'll show you how. Unfortunately, the sad news is Satan has been successful in destroying many families through the dangerous—deceptive practice of Voodoo, Witchcraft and the Occult etc. But I have good news...This ends now. After thoroughly reading this chapter your eyes will be opened.

The Bible says: "Satan deceives the whole world..." (Rev. 12:9). After reading all the previous chapters about Voodoo, I am sure that you're convinced that it is not a godly religion; it is a mystery pagan religion and God detests it and its practices. And His command to you is "Turn away from such practices." Now that we have established that here's what to do:

Confess your sins to God—in this segment I am addressing both the professed Christian and the Voodoo practitioner.

At that stage you must have a personal revival. What is impossible for you God will do but you must act quickly and confess your sins to the Lord in the name of Jesus (Yehoshua) Christ. That is the only name given unto name for salvation; the only way but it is the sure Way. Confession is almost always a hard thing to make especially when one is guilty. Unlike man's court system God's court system is different. He (God) does not condemn you but sets you free and restores you. He does not overwhelm you with shame but accept you as an adoptive son or daughter the moment you invite Christ in your life through genuine repentance. You can't confess to God on your own strength or ability, you must do it in the name of Jesus the only savior of mankind. The personal revival is very crucial for both the saved and the unsaved. It is an indication that your life has been offensive to the Lord and that you need to make a complete turnaround.

If you find the following in your life, you must pray and ask God to change you.

You've become:

Unthankful—you complain more than you thank God for His faithfulness; therefore, you become bitter at yourself and toward God. Instead, you should develop an attitude of thankfulness toward the Lord like David and Paul did (Psalms 95:2; 100: 4; 105:1; I Thessalonians 5:18; Ephesians 5:20).

Neglecting Bible study—you think you know more than anybody else; therefore, developing a lack of interest in attending study. Money has replaced God. While it is not wrong to work but if you're self employed you can arrange your schedule to attend Bible study but if you were never the type, prior to working, never or rarely attend bible study, don't use your business as an excuse for not showing up. If you choose TV, the Internet or pleasure over bible study, you need a revival.* Satan has put a hook on you, deceiving you to think that you are right, you just having some "me" time and God is not angry at you. You convince yourself that after all, the pastor's teaching is no longer good, you've heard him before why bother going or the devil can suggest to you that the pastor is not going to be present it is just another leader appointed to do the job just stay home. Once you fall into that trap you are challenging God's authority because if the pastor places someone else in charge of anything at your local church, he/she deserves the same respect you show to the pastor. If you challenge their authority you are acting like Lucifer, pride has invaded you heart and think that, just like him, you can do better. Be careful for you know what happened to the enemy when he tried that trick...Be careful.

---

* By revival, I don't mean going to a massive gathering filled with thrilled and excitement; rather a serious repentance toward God.

Note: If you're at a place where the whole truth of the Bible is not being taught, you must leave that place. You will be better off staying home and study on your own or with someone who has no barrier of doctrine or denomination. The Bible should never be taught according to one's specific Denomination. Unfortunately, many churches are doing this, deceiving God's people.

Stubbornness—if you keep doing the same things over and over and expect a different result you are stubborn. Most people think that their ways are always better and if you don't choose their way of doing things you have a spiritual problem; something is wrong with your spirit; you are not in alignment. Friends, it is not about what someone says but it's about what God says and thinks. Religious people will torture you and make you feel guilty because you are not like them. You were made an original don't let someone turns you into a copy. Stubbornness can cause you to be misled by your peers, your leaders and anyone else. It can cause you to deceive yourself and sin against God Almighty. In fact, let's call it for what it is: stubbornness is a sin, period.

Lack of love for God—if you love God, you will obey Him (I John 2:4-5); you will not be faithless because it displeases the Lord. You will not slander, hate, or bad mouth you neighbor. Lack of love for God drives you to be a friend of the world rather than being a friend of God; you need to change that. Idol worship is sin. In Voodoo the worshipping of these idols are rampant. We can't live in an open rebellion to God and expect Him to bless us.

Lack of love for lost souls—the Bible says, "He who saves soul is wise." In what way (s) are you contributing in emptying hell and filling up heaven? Are you using your gifts and talents to work for God? Do you just burry your talents and wait until the Lord returns? You have a part to play. If you are involved in anything other than the culture of God, you need to turn around right now and do the right thing.

Derelict of family duties—despising your wife and children are detestable. You need to pray for and with them. Your wife is not an object; just because you pay all the bills in the house doesn't mean you own her and do what pleases you only...This is selfish. And wife just because you make more money than your husband or have advanced degree in school doesn't mean you're his master. You must still submit and respect him. Voodoo practitioners at most lack a sense of family duty. Their master, Satan is not about family, because it reminds him of God whom he hates. A Voodoo practitioner will have a wife and multiple girlfriends on the side and vice versa for the female; they will involve with many men. Be careful not to judge the Vodouisants if you're doing the same things they are doing.

Forgive—in order to be free you must forgive. If you've given up Voodoo, Occult or Witchcraft etc, you must forgive those who have hurt you. Lack of forgiveness in your heart will cause Satan to use you as his factotum.

He will always have something to tug at from you; this will be his chain with which he binds you. Forgiveness is for you. When you resent someone you are hurting yourself while he is having a good time not thinking of you. You have to learn to let go and let God. I've been hurt by church folks. Once, I made a mistake and fell into temptation. My involvement with a particular girl at the church surfaced and turned out ugly. At the time my involvement came out I no longer had intimate relation with that girl we were just friends. Let me remind you also that we were never boyfriend, girlfriend type.

My talents and gifts attracted her to me and silly me then, I bit into the bait and got involved sexually with her. She wanted to still hanging around, introduced me to her family not as a boyfriend (because I wasn't) but as a brother in the church and asked if I could help her nieces in school to which I responded yes and have helped them with homework, help them with the Bible etc. After about a year I started dating a wonderful girl (who is now my wife). Upon hearing that, she was furious, thinking I should be hers.

Though she knew and I insisted many times over we have nothing going on, in fact, in public and in private over and over I kept on reminding her we are just friends. She would sexual approach asking for sex and I would turn her down. But anyways, she claimed that she was convicted by the Holy Spirit, went to my former pastors' wife under the advices of her supposed best friend at the congregation, who was not really her best friend, and lashed out about us. Later on, she went to different other people including to my current wife whom I was courting then to lie to them through her teeth. I denied my involvement with her because I felt that it was the past. When the pastor confronted me about I said no. So I lied to him which gave that woman leverage on me after I admitted to the pastor yes it did happen but we were never boyfriend/girlfriend. I still got Facebook messages to prove it. Her infatuation for me got her to accuse me of other things which I don't have room here to describe. But just wait on my upcoming Memoir and you will read all about it.

When that story got out; those who were hearing about it from her now had a stone to cast on me. It was ridiculous. Those people, I used to eat with them, laugh with them, calling me brother, helped them when they were in need and all of a sudden I was the most hated one in their eyes. They can talk about love all they want to now, but the fact of the matter is, they hated me, they were jealous of me and I knew this from the people they used to talk about me with. The things I was hearing said about me were unthinkable; outright lies were being poured on me. Nevertheless, with all the right that I had to revenge myself, I didn't and trust me friends, I could have. But I let God handle the situation and He did a great job as always. What I should've lost I've gained. I am at peace and I can walk with my head held high. I have forgiven them and did not seek revenge. Though I was stoned by those who had no right to stone me, their life was no better than mine but because they have magnified my sins over theirs they felt that they were better. Nevertheless, I forgave them. Friends if you want God to be on your side, you must forgive others and you must forgive yourself, God is not through with you yet. When people reject you God will accept you.

Now to the Voodoo practitioners; once you give up that practice you have to forgive. I know in Voodoo it is an eye for an eye and a tooth for a tooth; but you can no longer live like this. Hatred will never end and blood will never stop shedding. The chain breaker must stop shedding innocent blood. You are a new creature in Christ once you've crossed over to the good side. You are light and no longer in darkness. The old has gone and the new has come. When you seek revenge you will not have peace. Whatever relief you have will be temporary.

Next you must repent—repentance is a complete turnaround from what you used to do that used to often God. Voodoo practice dishonors God and offends Christ. You shall have no other gods and you can only come to the One true God only through Jesus Christ; not by means of some spirits. Once you repent, don't go back to it. I've seen/known many professed Christians go back to Voodoo to only their demise. Your repentance must be sincere. You cannot let others inveigle you into going back to Voodoo or to let fear, sickness or illness bring you back. Some former practitioners have unfortunately gone back. I knew a lady who went all the way to Haiti catch a flight so as to go seek healing from a Voodoo priest because she believed that someone had casted a spell on her. She was a professed Christian going to church every Sunday and brought her kids with her but when things got tough she basically renounce Jesus and sought other means for healing. Dear reader, you should not let that happen to you. Once you repent, Jesus is faithful enough to take care of all, yes all of your needs for nothing can separate you from the love of God the Father.

Lastly, you must renounce—repent is to show Satan and his acolytes that you are no longer their factotum while renouncing is to break the legal contract that you may have given Satan over your life or that he may have acquired through family liaison. You must do so in the name of Jesus. At the hearing of that name he has no choice but to bow and you will be free and free indeed.

Beware of spiritual bondage

Many may refer to spiritual bondage as something that only happens in Voodoo, Witchcraft, Secret Societies etc; however, there is also spiritual bondage within the body of Christ. Many false teachers have crept in unaware in the *body* and have deceived many with erroneous doctrines under the radar of denomination. While the Bible warns (give scripture references) us of these false teachers, doctrines and denominations, lack of biblical knowledge causes quite a few believers to be in bondage (Revelation 12:9).

For example, I grew up as a Catholic but when I moved to the USA, I gave my life to Christ because I found out that Roman Catholicism was false because of so many doctrines/dogmas they hold dear to that are false (worshipping the Virgin Mary, Infant Baptism, believe in works to be saved, Masses for the dead, worshipping the dead as saint, removing from the Ten Commandments and more).

However, more deceptions were to come my way in the form of Pentecostalism that I just found out is also false. For nine years, after I got saved, I was part of a congregation that is Pentecostal; to tell you the truth though, they do have the foundation right. They do teach that man are sinners and that we need a savior; that salvation is through faith alone and Christ alone...it is Christ plus nothing that gives salvation (for by grace ye have been saved through...). Furthermore, they do teach about love, warning believers not to forsake the gathering of the brethren and many of them are sincerely nice people.

HOWEVER, if you got saved through a Pentecostal church and have already learned the foundation, you must leave right away...I will tell you right now:

1. Most Pentecostals (and I mean the leaders of big and small churches) believe that even if you're saved, you don't have the Holy Spirit working in you if you don't speak in TONGUES. That is a major lie. When I confronted my leaders about speaker in tongues about a year ago as I was revising this book, I was told that I am in error and that there are places he can go, I can't. When

I ask why, he said, "because you don't speak in tongues." I said, "really? I thought I only need Jesus and once I have Him, went through repentance, baptism etc, did I receive the Holy Spirit then?" He replied, "The disciples had Jesus, didn't they?" "why was it important then for Him to tell them to wait to receive power?" he added. And then he went to tell me about the time when Jesus blew air on the disciples and said, "receive the Holy Ghost." Because of that, his argument was, that the disciples had Jesus, they had the Holy Spirit but they did not have power until the day of Pentecost. So according to him the Holy Spirit was not given on the day of Pentecost.

Folks this is simply bad hermeneutic and I'll prove it to you because one day you will have to face a Pentecostal preacher who holds dearly to a false tongue not given by God but will try every excuse to make his belief fit the Bible.

Jesus indeed blew on the disciples and told them to receive the Holy Spirit...no doubt this is biblical because it is in the Bible, but what does it mean? This was a preparation for what would come on the day of Pentecost so that they (the disciples) would not fear at the actual giving of the Holy Ghost. Let's put that verse in its proper context. If John....is taken literally then John....is a lie. Here's what Jesus said to the disciple as they were sad at the hearing that He would go somewhere they cannot come:

But now I go my way to him that sent me; and none of you asketh me, whither goest thou? But because I have said these things unto you, sorrow hath filled your heart. Nevertheless I tell you the truth; it is expedient for you that I go away: for if I go not away, the Comforter will not come unto you; but if I depart, I will send him unto you. And when he is come, he will reprove the world of sin, and of righteousness, and of judgment. John 16: 5-8); read also John 14:26; 15:26).

The same John who told you He blew on them is telling you in the previous verses when the Holy Spirit will be given to them, and this is plain and clear as this can be. Would Jesus make a mistake not knowing when He would send the Holy Spirit? Did He have a new revelation after His death, burial and resurrection? Was He in a rush to give them the Spirit now, rather than on the day of Pentecost? The answer to these questions is an obvious, no. The reason so many Pentecostals hold so tenaciously to the Holy Spirit being given on the when Jesus blew on the disciples is because they want to exalt speaking in tongues as the gift to have. However, Paul clearly states that speaking in tongues is not the best gift nor the one to be desired (I Corinthians 14).

Another reason why I believe, according to the Bible that the Holy Spirit was not given when Jesus blew on them is the fact that not all of them were present in the room (show scripture). So now the question is, when did Thomas received the Holy Ghost? The Bible answers that in Acts 2, as they were all in the upper room; this is when the Holy Spirit descended on them and has never left; He is here as our Comforter, Advocate, guiding the believer in truth—leading him/her out of error. No one can be a Christian without the Holy Spirit.

Today's modern speaking in tongues is false. Look at Acts 2, the ones filled with Holy Ghost were speaking other people's native language that they did not learn but was instantly given to them. In an attempt to justify the false tongues, I was told that there three kinds of tongues. The one the disciples spoke in Acts, the one in I Corinthians 13 and 14. Again that teaching is false. Look closely at I Corinthians 14, Paul was rebuking the tongue talkers, he was calling them out on their display of immaturity; and that is the same message he is giving them today. If you ever visited a Pentecostal congregation you will quickly agree with me, everyone who claim to have that gift, though false by the way, will speak at the same time...no order at all. God can never be in any chaos or confusion, for He is not "the author of confusion."

2. Speaking in tongues locks the believer in a state of ecstasy, a false happiness and a temporary thrill. He is told by his pastor that he has something that the rest of common believers do not have. Meanwhile, he is deceived without even knowing it because he feels good to know

that he has power; not knowing that he is grieving the Holy Spirit; attributing to Him (Holy Spirit) a gift He did not give. This is spiritual bondage, thinking that you have something (power) and you don't; thinking you're serving God with your gift, but that gift is false because it was not given by God. So you will continually stay in your state of ecstasy, pride and arrogance that if not taken care of through humility and repentance upon receiving the knowledge of truth, can cause destruction. Hear this, if God did not give it to you then the devil did or is using your ignorance as an entrance door to manipulate you and cause you to do the same to others. Modern day SPEAKING IN TONGUES IS FALSE.

Speaking in tongues or at least the modern day tongue is not unique to Pentecostals as many other groups also can speak in tongues: Hindus (in the practice of Kundalini), some Catholics, some Mormons, devil-possessed spiritists, heathen witch doctors in Africa and Asia[37]. And in Haiti, voodoo spirits speak tongue ALL THE TIME. Pentecostalism is also false in the sense that they are calling the Holy Spirit to come down, in fact begging Him. Well the Spirit has not left since Pentecost. Furthermore, they love to tarry and wait, having tarry meeting, this also is a bad hermeneutic. The disciples were indeed asked by our Lord to tarry and wait because that was the first and only time the

Holy Spirit was going to make a great introduction in that fashion. Pentecost will not be repeated for Jesus said, "I will never leave you nor forsake you." By giving the believer the Comforter, He has kept His promise. Tarry meetings, calling down on the Holy Spirit are just man made, not true. You may feel good doing so, but it is in vain.

Another way people are kept in bondage is with the word, LOVE, used out of context or for mind control purposes.

Many denominations will preach about love, promote love and in a way embrace love. But that word also is being abused and used for mind control. I would admit that the foundation of Christianity is love, no doubt but loving someone also includes telling them the whole truth no matter how painful it is. It encompasses preaching the whole Gospel without barrier of denomination or doctrinal statements. We do not love our brothers and sisters in Christ when we conceal truth to promote a false teaching just because that teaching was done by one of our own. We are not called to defend heresies; we are called to stand for the truth by preaching the Gospel and teach believers everything the Lord has taught through His word.

"And Jesus came and spake unto them, saying, 'All power is given unto me in heaven and in earth. Go ye therefore, and teach all nations, baptizing them in the name of the Father, and of the Son, and of the Holy

Ghost: Teaching them to observe all things whatsoever I have commanded you... -- Matthew 28:18-20

Here are some signs to know if you are in a spiritual bondage at your church:

- ✓ Your pastor claims that only he can hear from God, placing himself above everyone else as if he is Moses.

- ✓ Your pastor is constantly having a revelation from God for your life; telling you who to marry and to stay away from. (I've seen so many wrecked because of that behavior...many have gotten married, unequally yoke with another partner because their leader push them to do so).

- ✓ Your pastor claims that speaking in tongues is what get you closer to God. This is a lie, for obeying God and get in your word are what get you closer to God. In fact, tongues is the least of the gifts.

- ✓ Your pastor is using the Bible against you to preach against you if you disagree with his/her heresies.

- ✓ He is using the story of Moses and his sister to tell you that God is going to give you leprosy if you don't listen to him. This also is a bad hermeneutic or he is purposely seeking to control your mind.

✓ He is telling you to not touch God's anointed. Again bad hermeneutic, everyone true believer is anointed; if you're a Christian today, you have the same anointing as does every other true believer (I John 2:20, 27). In the Old Testament the Holy Spirit was given temporarily to the men of God so that they might carry out the task at hand. Today, we are filled with the Holy Ghost; He lives in the heart of the believer.

These are just a few example of the way you can be manipulated by your church leaders and I am persuaded that at least you've been a victim of at least two of these false teachings. Brethren, deception pervade the world and Satan deceives the whole world (Revelation 12:9). I admonish you to open your eyes in these last days, open your Bible (KJV) and study like you've never studied before, trust me you will discover great things that many pastors are not teaching in their congregation.

Chapter 11
Voodoo in the United States

For the time will come when they will not endure sound doctrine; but after their own lusts shall they heap to themselves teachers, having itching ears; and they shall turn away their ears from truth, and shall be turned unto fables.

2 Timothy 4:3,4

The United States of America is one of the most multicultural countries on planet earth. The rest of the world wants to come here, whether it is for financial reasons or for political freedom. Muslims throughout the Middle East, for example, have fled their homelands in the fear of persecution if one is converted to Christianity. They are all welcomed here by the government because the US understands the atrocities and hardships these people are facing over there. Women are abused excessively, and freedom of speech is nearly nonexistent for them. There are many immigrants from other countries, but I can mention only a few in this chapter.

Let me take Cuba, for example. The dictatorship of Fidel Castro has driven most of the population out of that country. The majority of them have migrated in the "Land of the Free." When they cannot take it anymore, they use all sorts of ways to get to the US, risking their lives in quest of a better life. Mexicans also are taking great risks every day, crossing the US border. Men, women, and children have come in great numbers throughout the years and are still doing so, all in the name of democracy and better living conditions than they have back home.

Joining these two countries, known for their immigrants to the United States, is Haiti. Many Haitians have lost their lives trying to come to the US. They ride on small or big boats in order to find out what life on the other side has to offer. Sadly, many men, women, children, and even babies don't survive the trips. Instead of making it here to earn money and provide for themselves and their families, they have become food for the sharks and other living creatures of the sea. Thousands of lives have been lost, and many of the ones who made it here, whether Haitians, Cubans, Mexicans, etc., have ghastly stories to tell of their illegal trips.

Because of the immigrants, the US has becoming a melting-pot country. Moreover, the newcomers have brought their own cultures, religions, and traditions into this land, particularly in States like New York, Florida, California, Louisiana, and Texas. Slaves from West Africa have brought voodoo practices to the US since the beginning of the slave trade, a dreadful time in history. The trade or voyage from Africa to the Americas was called the "Middle Passage." Records have documented over 30,000 voyages between these continents transporting slaves. Each voyage lasted from one to three months. Men were marked with red-hot iron and shackled under the deck during the whole voyage, whereas the women were continually raped by the traders and the boys were used for the pleasure of the sailors.

The ships could carry no more than 350 people according to regulations, but the wicked sailors broke the rule and carried more than 800 men, women, and children on board. They were forced to sleep in filthy conditions and lived in harsh, hot, insufferable circumstances.

Many of them died due to malnutrition, diseases, being tossed overboard, or suicide. Those trips were a most brutal, horrifying, and dehumanizing experience for the Africans. More Africans came to Brazil and the Caribbean than to the United States. In fact, only an estimated 5 percent of slaves came to North America. The majority of them were from the West African kingdom of Dahomey, from the Ewe and Fon groups. Voodoo in the US and the Caribbean came with them. Later on, in the early 1800s, other forms of voodoo, like the Haitian voodoo, crossed over into Louisiana.

Many people I speak with think of voodoo as something only Haitians practice. But voodoo is not only a Haitian religion. It is also practiced here in the US and in many South American and Caribbean countries, where African slaves from the Yoruba religion were imported. Below is a list of the variations of voodoo throughout the Caribbean and South America.

- **Voodoo or Vodou** in Haiti (**Vodoun** from West Africa)

- **Santeria** in Cuba

- **Shango** in Trinidad

- **Camdomble** in Brazil

- **Kumina** in Jamaica.

In Miami, there are many voodoo stores; they are called *botanica*. This comes from the Greek word *botanikos*, meaning "plants." Haitian voodoo rituals all sorts of plants and other natural, earthly things are used to serve many purposes. They use the leaves of the plants for medicine or to cast evil spells, even to the point of killing. There are trees that are forbidden to be cut down in Haiti, like the tree under which the ceremony of the wood cayman was conducted. Many pastors and evangelicals have been chased from the location of that tree and threatened with their lives if they came to pray against that tree.

People worship trees in Haiti. In fact, I had a voodoo priest who gave me a prayer to recite if I ever traveled at night and couldn't make it home. That prayer was to be addressed to any tree for protection and shelter. Trees are used for many different purposes in Haiti. I know for a fact that in a neighborhood called Bel Air, in Cap-Haitian, a big tree there serves as a tribunal at night for the zombies to be judged by their killers. People from the local environment are usually terrified to pass by late at night. There is sometimes a ghastly smell coming from that tree, and people's blood shivers when come near.

Anyone who lives in Miami has at least seen a voodoo store. Some probably didn't know what they were until they read this chapter, but inside they are horrifying and spooky, and the smell is unpleasant. You don't need a Ph.D. to know that the devil lives in these places. These stores sell things that are used in voodoo to kill, cast spells on people, and invoke evil spirits. Yet, from what I know, there are no laws in Florida against the existence of these places. Next to the church where I am now a member, was a *botanica*. But after years of persistence in prayer, the place was shut down by the power of God. And it is now being used for an after-school program and summer camp, sponsored by The Children's Trust. I also had the privilege of working there with some wonderful kids and a great staff, all lovers of Jesus Christ. Darkness cannot stand light, and prayer is more powerful than magic; the glory of our Savior will overshadow the craftiness of the devil.

I feel that when it comes to the occult, the government stays silent and seems not to care at all. What is ironic is that this country embraces the motto "In God we trust," but the Ten Commandments are being taking off public schools. Furthermore, God says we can only have one master, and yet the US is allowing ungodly religions to exist right here. For example, the Church of Satan, created by Anton LaVey in 1966 in San Francisco, is free to practice its religion. The name itself says everything. I also believe that when it comes to the things of the devil, the US is too passive. It is time to say no to Harry Potter and books about Satanism and embrace the Word of God as a guide for our children in schools. The time is now to say no to witchcraft and accept Jesus. When the United States is giving voice to evil, this is not justice. When all these false religions exist, justice is not being served.

The First Amendment gives too much freedom of religion, especially to those who are practicing evil. I could not put it better than this Latin citation: *"Summum jus, summa injuria,"* meaning, "An extreme justice is an extreme injustice." It is injustice when a society stays quiet about false teachings and doctrines and talks about balance in the justice system, when in fact they are promoting immorality. You can't talk about justice when you know a group of people is about to go to hell, and you do nothing to try to stop it. A country built on biblical principles shouldn't allow any ungodly teachings to be taught, especially to our kids, the next generation.

Voodoo ceremonies are still being conducted in the backyard of cities like Miami, Boston, New York, and New Orleans. The cemeteries are frequently visited at night by those who love to invoke the dead. In Miami, there are many voodoo ceremonies and animal sacrifices made to the devil by voodoo practitioners. This is wrong!

When hatred arises in places where mostly Cubans and Haitians are working, the solution to an argument is to go to witchcraft. They will cause their coworkers to get fired or cast a spell to harm them. One gentleman, probably in his late forties said this: "If I ever get fired, I will kill whoever causes that." He further added that, he is deep into magic and that it is nearly impossible for a boss to fire him from a job.

Witchcraft in any part of the world brings shame, quarrels, turmoil, and division. Whatever name you give it, it will never equal the love of God. Any family where the Word of God is not the final authority is subject to falling apart. Husbands will mistreat wives, wives will be disrespectful to their husbands, siblings will rise against one another, and children will be raised with no guidance.

My best friend, whom I have known for a long time, encountered many hardships from his own family. His sisters didn't like him very much because he did not have a job. They blamed him for everything bad that happened in the house, even when he had no clue about the issue. Each time the bills had to be paid, it was like living in hell for him because of his sisters' mouths. My friend has a caring heart, and his family knew it. Everything he has he will share with others, but his own family was blinded by the love of money; thus they were lured away by their evil minds.

Many times, my friend came close to going to jail because of the company his sisters kept, but God protected him. People came and put their cocaine in the house; but when my friend complained to his sisters, his words were not heard. They ridiculed him instead and made him feel less than nothing. They had hatred in their hearts for him for no reason at all. One day a neighbor, a young lady, came and told lies on my friend to his sisters, stirring up trouble. Without even finding out the truth by giving him a chance to talk, the oldest one asked him to leave the house like a dog. With no warning and no place to stay, my friend had to leave immediately. He had just found a job one week prior to that incident; so with no money in his hands, sorrow burning him inside, and tears flooding down his cheeks, he desperately called upon God, and the always faithful Father heard his prayer and answered him. Another friend of ours gave him shelter. Everything went well. Each day he sought God's face, asking him for help, and Jehovah always provided for him, blessing him in many ways.

After two months, he moved out on his own, and the Lord promoted him, giving him a better job. He forgave whoever hurt him and let go of the pain, for he understood that his future is in the hands of the Almighty. He always gives God thanks and glory, recognizing Him as the source for his happiness and peace today and for the rest of his life.

Friends, the God of Abraham, Isaac, and Jacob loves you. He doesn't want you to suffer because you are His children. He took Joseph from the pit and out of slavery to put him in the palace in Egypt as one of the most powerful men in the world. He saved the world from hunger by using Joseph. With God there is no defeat!

The practice of voodoo is detrimental to a land, a family, and its followers. The United States is no stranger to the world of witchcraft and other unholy teachings. Your children are being exposed to satanic books. Certain movies and TV shows are destructive and impure to your minds and your children's. The devil is doing whatever he can to find people to join him in hell, and he is targeting you and me, the very apple of God's eye, because he wants to avenge his fall from heaven. The government will not and cannot save you; it is a personal decision between you and Jesus.

There are many voodoo priests here in the US, and the people who consult them do so to find luck, protection, money, and power. Most of the time they never get what they are looking for, but if by chance they happen to get money or power, it is for their own destruction. Why? Satan cannot give what he doesn't have, and the voodoo priest is an agent of Satan; therefore all he has to offer are lies. I had a friend in the North Miami area who operated as a voodoo priest, even though he was not one. He used it as a scheme to get women and to make money off of people who rely on superstition. Blacks, whites, and Hispanics all have been victimized by his schemes.

Many people in the US are willing to do anything to make their dreams come true, and many of them now believe that voodoo can help them live the American dream. Immorality and ignorance invade their hearts and cause them to act foolishly. Many voodoo believers, therefore, have been deceived. This con artist that I mentioned explained how he slept with the girls who came to him. Many of them came to take a "good-luck shower" so that they could win the lotto or win at the casino. Before he started doing any procedure, they had to do sexual favors for him. Because these women were so hungry for money, they were willing to do anything. In addition to looking for luck, these young women also relied on voodoo either to save their marriages if they were married or to find a husband if they were single. I can assure you, they will never find true love and happiness like that. Instead, it is the cancer of hatred and deception that will consume their hearts.

Although the gospel of Jesus Christ is being preached around the globe, especially here in America where we can go on line and read the Bible or listen to a sermon on a podcast or TV, people still are living in ignorance. And they are doing so willingly. They choose to misunderstand freedom and free will, not knowing that this is a wrong path to take and is a road to destruction and death. Voodoo is not the only thing that can destroy a great nation, but there are many other secret groups with hidden agendas working in concert with it.

Satan always has a leader or a small group of people influenced to do his work. The devil seduces them with money and power to do his will, which is to mislead people, even the children of the Most High, by way of apocryphal teachings. It is the work of Satan when children are forbidden to read the Word of God in school but are forced to read books about the occult. It is a danger to the American society and immoral when the justice system is silent in some states that support homosexuality. Marriage always has been and always will be between a man and a woman. God didn't create "Adam and Sam" or "Eve and Esther." He created Adam and Eve, the first married couple, to multiply and populate the earth. The Bible says, "So God created man in his own image, in the image of God created he him; male and female created he them. And God blessed them, and God said unto them, Be fruitful, and multiply, and replenish the earth, and subdue it: and have dominion over the fish of the sea, and over the fowl of the air, and over every living thing that moveth upon the earth" (Gen. 1:27-28).

Moreover, it is absurd and ludicrous to throw the Ten Commandments out of the school system and replace them with ungodly books. Most people think that we do not live by the law anymore, so it is not a problem to ignore God's law. Wrong! Jesus Christ Himself said this: "Think not that I am come to destroy the law, or the prophets: I am not come to destroy, but to fulfill" (Matt. 5:17).

Again, I think the devil is very happy with the justice system, which allows abortion clinics to remain open. Each day, scores of babies are being murdered. Thousands of innocent lives are lost daily and millions yearly, yet no one said anything to put an end to this cruelty. It is hideous!

As I mentioned before, voodoo is not of God. Wherever it is practiced there is no joy and no peace. Here in Miami, where I live, there are gang members, either born here with Caribbean backgrounds or born in the Caribbean, who rely on voodoo for protection. Sadly, some of them have lost their lives, and others are now serving time behind bars. Voodoo will tell you, "Go act the fool, for you are untouchable," but in the end, you will be a victim of that deception if you listen to it. I know of many who have lost loved ones. To this day they are grieving over those losses or suffer because their dear sons or daughters are incarcerated. In the US, just as in Haiti, voodoo is always this: If someone doesn't like you, your success, your children, or something you've done, he or she will try to harm you by means of magic.

It is nearly impossible for two businesses owned by Haitians to survive side by side. There is always competition and jealousy. Their thinking is, "If your business exists, mine won't make any money; thus I shall destroy yours." Right here in Miami, most business owners from the Haitian community put weird voodoo articles in their stores and restaurants in order to protect their assets so that others don't destroy them with magic. Every morning, I witness them glorifying the devil before opening their stores. They sprinkle water in the front doors and pour out coffee, which is a form of salutation and praise to the lwas in Haitian voodoo.

All of this is idolatry, which is condemned by the Word of God. If we turn away from God's Word, we are not being humble; we are being prideful, thinking that we can make it on our own. Pride creates greed, and this will be manifested in jealousy, which will later develop into all sorts of immoralities, even murder. That's why the Holy Bible advises us to "Mortify therefore your members which are upon the earth; fornication, uncleanness, inordinate affection, evil concupiscence, and covetousness, which is idolatry" (Col. 3:5).

All in all, voodoo, sorcery, witchcraft, and any ungodly religion or any other variation of these teachings and practices are wrong no matter where on earth they are found. Those who are still involved in them are doing so in order to acquire power, something that is ephemeral. True power comes from God; this is an undeniable sempiternal truth. Any form of authority that is not from God can lead to destruction and cause those in charge to commit abuse and injustice, just as in those many countries where slavery was carried practiced. We saw in chapter 2 how the colonists pillaged Hispaniola, destroyed its first inhabitants, and enriched their countries in the process through the most dehumanizing form of slavery. It is clear that these people had power, but they did not have the love of God dwelling in their hearts. They used religion as an instrument to create fear in the land and to justify their treatment of the captives.

Christians must be vigilant and prayerful in order not to be deceived. And those who are not followers of Jesus Christ need to quickly switch sides because time is at hand; the return of Christ is imminent, and you don't want to be left out. Voodoo cannot save you, your religion, pastor, priest, or family cannot save you. It is between you and Jesus.

Remember, we do not own anything, but we are stewards over everything the Lord has placed on the earth to ensure our well-being. Therefore, God is not pleased when we are destroying His properties and each other. We certainly wouldn't be happy if someone were destroying our possessions, and the Father feels the same way. The Bible says, "The earth is the Lord's, and the fullness thereof; the world, and they that dwell therein" (Ps. 24:1). Stop worshiping the creatures, and worship the Creator. Do not fear those who are doing evil, for God will be a refuge to you if you call on Him; He loves you and wants to save your soul more than anything in the world. I will leave with these words from 1 John 3:1: "Behold, what manner of love the Father hath bestowed upon us, that we should be called the sons of God: therefore the world knoweth us not, because it knew him not."

Conclusion

Friends, tomorrow is not promised and you will be dead longer than you lived. If you don't believe just look at a grave the next time you go to a funeral at the cemetery and see the little dash between the time of birth and death of that person buried; you will quickly get the point. You might see something like this: Mr. John Doe, from 1930-1970. That is, this person was born in 1930 and died in 1970 and guess what the year is now 2014 and going. So this individual has been dead longer than he lived; I am sure you got the point.

However, death is not the end, it's just the begin of a new "life" with God or without Him; without him would be what the Bible describe as the second death (Rev 21: 8). You may think that you're a good person and there is no way God will reject you... well no one is good for we are all sinners (Romans 3: 23) and the wages (payment) for our sins is death (Romans 6:23), not partial death but complete death and torment. However, God in His perfect love gave us sinners a free gift, but very costly to Him (John 3: 16). Salvation cannot be earned because there is no one righteous, so none can boast, no matter how many good works or how moral you think you are. "For by grace are ye saved through faith; and that not of yourselves: it is the gift of God: Not of works, lest any man should boast"(Ephesians 2: 8-9).

If you do not have Jesus, you are not living; you are a dead spirit walking in the flesh. As you have read, I spent a very long time being deceived, and that did not bring joy, peace, or happiness. No matter what I could accomplish with demonic power, it brought nothing but vile experiences.

Jesus Christ came and saved me. He made a trade with me taking all I had (sins) and gave me all He had (joy, peace, hope and above all, eternal life). Dear readers, I did exactly that. And guess what; I got the best out of the deal. I had nothing, and He has everything forever. You can't tell me that this deal is not sweet!

Today you have a chance to make the same trade. Will you agree and jump on it? I think you should, but I can't make the decision for you; it is between you and Him.

Today, if you read the above mentioned information about salvation and fully understand it, you have a choice to make. You can either reject or accept it; I pray you choose the latter. Not one person can make the decision for you. NO other name can save you, not Erzulie, Damballah, Buddha, Krishna etc, for "Neither is there salvation in any other: for there is none other name under heaven given among men, whereby we must be saved" (Acts 4:12). The only name given is Jesus Christ. "Wherefore God also hath highly exalted him, and given him a name which is above every name: That at the name of Jesus every knee should bow, of things in heaven, and things in earth, and things under the earth; And that every tongue should confess that Jesus Christ is Lord, to the glory of God the Father" (Philippians 2: 9-11).

So you see, it's only faith in Jesus Christ that saves; you can do nothing, nothing at all of your own strength to be saved. Remember salvation is a free gift from God. According to the Bible, after you recognize that you're a sinner and as such you deserve to die but you can escape that if you sincerely do this: "That if thou shalt confess with thy mouth the Lord Jesus, and shalt believe in thine heart that God hath raised him from the dead, thou shalt be saved. For with the heart man believeth unto righteousness; and with the mouth confession is made unto salvation" (Romans 10: 9-10). Dear reader, don't be afraid to come to God with a repentant heart for you do not want the outcome of Revelation 21:8 in your next life. "But the fearful, and unbelieving, and the abominable, and murderers, and whoremongers, and sorcerers, and idolaters, and all liars, shall have their part in the lake which burneth with fire and brimstone: which is the second death."

If you're ready to embrace Jesus and receive your free gift of salvation, you must repent with a sincere heart and your life will never be the same. I trust that you understand that your life here on earth is ephemeral. No matter how long you live here, you will be dead longer than you lived. If you go to the cemetery and visit some tombs, you'll be shocked to see this proof as only a – separates the time of birth and death of all individuals. For example, Georges Washington has been dead longer than he lived; however God, through His Son Jesus Christ, is the only one who can resurrect your mortal body and give you eternal life.

Therefore, if you have willingly and sincerely repented of your sins, you've become a new creature. It will not get easier but you will be at peace. You will be persecuted (John 15:20) for your faith in Christ particularly from those who knew your past, but don't fear them because the joy you'll experience with the Lord even in the midst of trouble and persecution will be incomparable. Welcome to your new family! Now that you have received Christ as your personal savior, don't hesitate to contact me so I can help you in your walk with the Lord to become a true disciple of Christ because your new task now is to go and teach all nations about the things of the Lord, teach them to obey God and baptize them in the name of the Father, the Son and of the Holy Spirit. (Matthew 28:19-20).

I'd love to connect with you, if this book has changed your life, please shoot me an email and I'll take it from there: info@frantztheauthor.com or write me at:

Frantz Michel

P.O. BOX 600342

North Miami Beach, FL. 33160

[1] J.J. Rousseau, The Social Contract, trans. Maurice Cranston (London : Penguin Classics) p. 52

[2] *Encarta ® World English Dictionary,* 1998-2004

[3] The original text was in French, my translation. Cited by par Rosa Amelia Plumelle Uribé, la férocité blanche, des Non-blancs aux Non-aryens. Editions Albin Michel, 2001

[4] http://www.abnihilo.com/

[5] Le mont des oliviers, *Comment composer mon devoir français,* Vingtième Edition

[6] Ibid

[7] Ibid

[8] Frantz Michel, *Can God Save Haiti?,* p. 12

[9] http://archives.cnn.com/2002/ALLPOLITICS/04/16/column.bill press/index.html

[10] http://www.teachinghearts.org/drf04historynotes.html

[11] *Rescued from Hell* [Parole de Vie Publishing House, 1996], 64

[12] *Harrap's French and English Dictionary,* 2004

[13] *La dignité du livre et devoirs du Prêtre* 12:2 ; see http://www.teachinghearts.org/drf04historynotes.html

[14] Daniels, D. W. (2006). *Babylon Religion: How a Babylonian goddess became the Virgin Mary.* Ontario, CA: Chick Publications, p. 155

[15] Ibid

[16] Ibid

[17] Ibid

[18] Gregory Toussaint, *Jezebel Unveiled,* GEM Publishing House, Miami, FL, 2008 p.56

[19] : http://en.wikipedia.org/wiki/Isis

[20] Daniels, D. W. (2006). *Babylon Religion: How a Babylonian goddess became the Virgin Mary,* p. 38. Ontario, CA: Chick Publications

[21] Icke, D. (1999). *The Biggest Secret* (2nd ed.). p. 53. Wildwood, MO: Bridge of Love Publications

[22] David W. Daniels, Babylon Religion: How a Babylonian goddess became the Virgin Mary, Chick Publications, CA, 2006, p. 81

[23] Ibid p. 81

[24] Icke, *The Biggest Secret* [Updated Second Edition], Bridge of Love Publications USA, Wildwood, MO, 1999, p. 55.)

[25] cited in Daniels, 2006, p. 46.

[26] Daniels, D. W. (2006). Babylon Religion: How a Babylonian goddess became the Virgin Mary. p.82. Ontario, CA: Chick Publications

[27] Ibid., p. 82

[28] see Daniels, *Babylon Religion*, p. 82.

[29] Hislop [1858], *The Two Babylons*, quoted by David W. Daniels in, *Babylon Religion: How a Babylonian goddess became the Virgin Mary*, Chick Publication, CA, 2006, p.34

[30] Ibid p. 74

[31] Ibid p. 74

[32] *See http://www.lefloridien.com/div.html*

[33] Haitian Penal Code, article 249 ; see http://www.themystica.com/mystica/articles/z/zombies.html

[34] http://www.thekkel.com/epiloguehtml

[35] http://en.wikipedia.org/wiki/Columbine_High_School_massacre

[36] http://en.wikipedia.org/wiki/Virginia_Tech_massacre

[37] John R. Rice, *The Charismatic Movement,* quoted here: http://dividedbytruth.org/FD/sitnnc.htm